DUTCH OVEN DINNERS

DUTCH OVEN DINNERS

A Cookbook for Flavorful Meals
Made in Your Favorite Pot

JANET A. ZIMMERMAN

ROCKRIDGE
PRESS

Interior and Cover Designer: Emma Hall
Art Producer: Tom Hood
Editor: Lauren Ladoceour
Production Editor: Mia Moran

Photography © Elysa Weitala 2020, food styling by Victoria Woollard, cover; Gareth Morgans/StockFood, pp ii, iii; Nadine Greeff/Stocksy, pp vi, xiv; Leigh Beisch/Stockfood, pp xi, 100; Great Stock!/Stockfood, pp 12, 54; Gräfe & Unzer Verlag/Jana Liebenstein/Stockfood, p. 20; Eising Studio/Stockfood, p. 30; News Life Media/Stockfood, pp 36, 70; Jonathan Gregson/Stockfood, p. 44; Bauer Syndication/Stockfood, pp 50, 80; The Picture Pantry/Stockfood, p. 62; Matthias Neubauer/Stockfood p. 74; Bill Kingston/Stockfood, p. 86; Darren Muir/Stocksy, p. 90; Gräfe & Unzer Verlag/Thorsten Suedfels/Stockfood, pp 96, 110; Darlina Kopcock/Stocksy, p. 106; Heather Ogg/Stockfood, p. 114
Author photo courtesy of Court Mast

ISBN: Print 978-1-64739-730-2
eBook 978-1-64739-432-5
R0

To Dave, who made sheltering in place enjoyable.

CONTENTS

CHAPTER THREE: Eight-Ingredient Showstoppers 31

CHAPTER FOUR: One-Pot Favorites 51

CHAPTER FIVE: Original Slow Cookers 71

INTRODUCTION

For more years than I care to admit, I worked in a cookware store, where one of my favorite duties was helping couples with their wedding registry lists. I always tried to guide them toward good, solid choices in outfitting their kitchen, and one of my first suggestions was invariably a Dutch oven. It was never a hard sell—who doesn't want a gorgeous, durable, and versatile pot that makes cooking such a pleasure?

I also practiced what I preached. I have owned Dutch ovens since I was able to afford my first cookware set from Le Creuset. The beautiful blue pots quickly became my most used vessels, as I discovered just how much they could do. I did, of course, use them for soups, stews, and braises, but they also filled in the gaps in my modest stash. I didn't have a wok, so I used them for stir-frying. I didn't have any other big pots, so I cooked pasta and steamed vegetables in them. I certainly couldn't afford a deep fryer, so they stood in on those occasions when I was in the mood for fish and chips.

Through the years, of course, my cupboards have filled up, but my Dutch ovens— which now include red and yellow in addition to my original blue pots—have continued to see frequent use. And as my kitchen has evolved, so, too, has my cooking style. I've gone through stages where I cooked elaborate meals for friends and family, stages where I needed to get dinner ready fast, and stages where my main concern was cooking from a limited pantry (having to lug groceries up a steep hill makes you think twice about what ingredients make the cut).

Maybe the greatest thing about a Dutch oven is how it can fit in with any cooking style. Yes, you can use it when you've got lots of time on the weekend and are in the mood for a slow-cooked meal. You can use it when you're having company and want a fancier dinner. But you can also use it when your loved ones are hungry and you want to get dinner on the table in less than an hour. You can even put it to work when all you have is a handful of ingredients.

And never forget, a Dutch oven is beautiful enough to serve from, so it can cut way down on cleanup. Many of the recipes in this book are for complete meals in one pot. Dinner doesn't get much easier than this!

So whether you're craving Spicy Orange Beef and Broccoli (page 15), Sweet and Spicy Glazed Salmon with Bok Choy (page 43), or one-pot comfort food like the Mustard-Spiked Beef Stew (page 63), you and your Dutch oven can make it happen. In the mood for slow-cooked Pork Ribs Cacciatore (page 84) or elegant Crab and Asparagus Risotto (page 94)? You guessed it! Your Dutch oven will do you proud. You can even use it for delicious side dishes—how much better can it get?

I hope after reading through this book, you'll be as excited with your Dutch oven as I am with mine.

CHAPTER ONE

Dinner Goes Dutch

"What's for dinner?" It's an age-old question that never seems to have an easy answer. But it doesn't have to be difficult. If you have a Dutch oven (and this book!), you'll never have to wonder again. That versatile pot can mean the difference between dreading and loving the evening meal. With a Dutch oven, you'll have easy, seemingly endless dinner options that will turn cooking from a chore into a joy.

DINNER'S FAVORITE POT

These days, there are a lot of convenient ways to put dinner on the table. Between frozen pizzas, delivery, takeout, and ready-cooked meals from our favorite markets, there's always something close at hand if your only goal is to eat. But many of us don't want that—at least, we don't want it all or even most of the time. We want to cook and enjoy an evening meal with our family and friends. Dinner is the one time in the day when we can catch up, spend time together, and share a home-cooked meal.

If that description fits you, this book can help turn your good intentions into reality. With your Dutch oven and a few kitchen tools, the recipes in this book will give you great ideas for complete meals with less fuss and more time to enjoy eating together.

Imagine cooking up chicken and white bean chili, orange beef and broccoli, or steamed cod on a bed of vibrant vegetables in 30 minutes. Imagine making Mexican-style stuffed peppers or spinach and mushroom pasta with just a handful of ingredients. Imagine preparing a full meal with just your Dutch oven—pot roast or roasted chicken—and serving it right in the same beautiful pot. All those possibilities are within your reach.

Sure, it takes a little planning, a little practice, and a little time. But once you discover how wonderful a home-cooked dinner can be, you'll begin to look forward to the time with your family and friends around the table and the oohs and ahhs as they dig in.

Even if your schedules don't always let you sit down at the same time, these recipes can still make modern dinners more enjoyable. Most of them keep warm and reheat well for those nights when you can't relax together but still want to serve healthy, home-cooked dinners. No matter what your dinner style, you'll have it made.

MAKING THE MOST OF YOUR DUTCH OVEN

In the early days of the American colonies, Dutch ovens were a kitchen workhorse. Their durability and versatility made them a valuable tool both inside farmhouse kitchens and outdoors at explorers' camps. In fact, Dutch ovens have been around for so long in so many kitchens, they might seem old-fashioned for today's cook. But if you believe the Dutch oven is just a quaint relic from more traditional times—a pot for cooking chili over the campfire—think again.

The very thing that made them so valuable on the farm—their versatility—is something we can all still take advantage of. In fact, some cooks would claim it's the only pot you need. Yes, it's great for braising or slow-cooking chili, but it has so many more uses. From boiling to baking to stir-frying, cooks rely on it to produce an amazing variety of meals, from Cajun gumbo to Italian pasta to Thai curries.

Boiling and Simmering

Dutch ovens excel at maintaining an even simmer without having to constantly adjust the heat under the pot. This is invaluable when making soups and stews, whether they cook for 30 or 90 minutes. And for dishes that require more heat, your Dutch oven can easily reach and keep a steady boil, so you can use it for cooking pasta, blanching vegetables, or reducing sauces.

Steaming

With the addition of a steamer basket, your Dutch oven can transform into a steamer. Its tight-fitting lid traps the steam and keeps the temperature constant to cook delicate vegetables, eggs, or potatoes for salad.

Frying

Whether you want to sear beef, shallow-fry chicken, or deep-fry fish fillets for a sandwich, a Dutch oven can do it all. Even heating and exceptional retention mean no hot spots when searing and a steady temperature when deep frying. With a little planning, you can even stir-fry in your pot.

Braising

Of all the kitchen techniques, braising is arguably your Dutch oven's greatest strength. It maintains low, even heat on the stovetop or in the oven, which results in meltingly tender meats and delectable sauces. From pork ribs cacciatore to pot roast to Moroccan chicken and sweet potatoes, you'll get perfectly delicious dinners with very little effort.

Roasting

In the oven, your sturdy pot can withstand the high heat of roasting, so it can take the place of a roasting pan, turning out beautiful meats and crisp roasted vegetables with equal ease. The radiant heat from the sides of the pot can even brown a whole chicken.

Baking

At lower oven temperatures, this versatile pot can act as a casserole dish, turning out creamy bakes with crisp brown toppings. And although it's beyond the scope of this book, you can even use it for baking desserts like apple crisp or no-knead bread.

GO HEAVY OR LIGHT

The Dutch oven in most of our kitchens, whether a wedding gift, inherited from Grandma, or saved up for, is cast iron coated with enamel. It's a heavyweight vessel, both literally and figuratively. A 5- to 6-quart Dutch oven will weigh 12 to 14 pounds. While this mass makes for wonderfully even cooking and heat retention, it also takes some muscle to lift. If that's not your style, there are lighter options that still provide most of the benefits of the classic cast-iron pot. The best alternative is enamel-coated cast aluminum, which weighs about 7 pounds but still gives you even heat distribution and retention. Anodized aluminum pots, usually with a nonstick interior, are another option, as are "clad" pots (stainless steel with an aluminum disk sandwiched on the bottom). Those both weigh a little less than the cast-aluminum pot, but they won't give you the even heat radiating from the sides of a heavier pot. They also heat faster than cast iron or aluminum, so you'll probably want to lower the heat on the stove top (oven temps can remain the same).

USEFUL TOOLS

The great thing about cooking with a Dutch oven is that you won't need a lot of special equipment. You've probably got most of these items in your kitchen already, and if you don't, they're inexpensive and easy to find.

Need to Have

SPATULA: A wok spatula or similar utensil in wood, bamboo, or silicone for stirring and deglazing. A wok spatula is angled on the bottom, with one curved side and one straight side, for getting into corners. While you can use metal utensils, they can scratch the enameled surface if you're not careful.

TONGS: Silicone-tipped long tongs for turning foods as you brown them prove more useful than a spatula. The deep sides of a Dutch oven keep splattering to a minimum, but they also make it easy to burn your arms if your utensils don't reach easily into the pot.

POTHOLDERS: Oven mitts or square potholders are essential. Standard Dutch ovens don't come with stay-cool handles, and even the stay-cool lid knob will heat up if you use your pot in the oven.

Nice to Have

FRY GEAR: If you plan to deep-fry in your Dutch oven, invest in a deep-fry thermometer and a "spider," a long-handled, basket-shaped strainer for removing food from the oil. A rack that fits in a sheet pan is great for draining foods after frying.

STEAMER: Collapsible metal or flexible silicone steamer inserts will let you steam green vegetables, eggs, and potatoes. I like silicone inserts since they don't scratch my pots, but some of the metal collapsible models now come with silicone-coated feet, which also work well.

COLANDER: If you want to cook pasta or boil potatoes in your Dutch oven, you'll need a colander or at least a large strainer to drain off the water.

FAT SEPARATOR: When you braise meat, it'll release fat into your sauce. You can simply blot or spoon this off, but a fat separator (which looks similar to a liquid measuring cup) does a more thorough job.

PANTRY BASICS

Nothing can make cooking dinner easier than a well-stocked pantry. It doesn't take a dedicated closet or even a whole cabinet; find room for a few staples where you can, and rest assured that a satisfying meal will always be at your fingertips.

Salt

Salt is probably the most common ingredient in my dinner recipes. Though it's a basic ingredient, it is a true workhorse in enhancing the flavor in even the simplest of recipes. I use Crystal Diamond brand kosher salt in all the recipes in this book. If you're using fine salt, use half as much as I call for.

Pepper

Like salt, ground black pepper is a pantry staple that simply plays a supporting role to the main ingredients found in recipes. If possible, use freshly ground black pepper; it has a much more pronounced taste and aroma than the pre-ground spice.

Oil

For tasks like searing meat or browning onions, I use a neutral vegetable oil, but I always have extra-virgin olive oil on hand for dishes that need a bit more flavor.

Vinegar

I like to keep a few varieties of vinegar on hand. Red or white wine vinegar, balsamic vinegar, sherry vinegar, and rice vinegar all make appearances in my recipes.

Spices

When you have a shelf of ground spices and dried herbs, you can elevate the ordinary to special. Keep them away from heat and light, and most will keep for months. Spice mixtures can be especially handy; I like a Cajun or Creole blend, chili powder, Italian herb mix, and curry powder.

Sauces

When I'm short on time and energy, a few high-quality commercial sauces can make dinner much easier and still delicious. I often turn to marinara sauce (I like Classico Riserva brand), salsas (my two favorites are Frontera's tomatillo and double-roasted tomato), store-bought pesto, and sun-dried tomato puree. For Asian-influenced recipes, I like a sweet Thai chili sauce, Thai curry pastes, hoisin sauce, soy sauce, and chili-garlic sauce—all of which can be found in the international foods aisle of most grocery stores.

Dried Rice, Beans, and Pasta

When you've got the time, a Dutch oven turns out fabulous bean dishes. I use dried black, white, red, and pinto beans as well as chickpeas. In this book's recipes, I use white rice rather than brown; long grain is fine, but jasmine and basmati are also great choices. For the Crab and Asparagus Risotto (page 94), you'll want Arborio or carnaroli rice. Several recipes in this book call for dried pasta—linguine, penne, farfalle (butterflies), and Chinese wheat noodles are among my standbys.

Canned Goods

As much as I like dried beans, when I'm in a hurry, I find canned beans to be invaluable for getting dinner on the table quickly. Other canned goods in my recipes include stock, tomatoes, coconut milk, chiles, and roasted nuts for garnishing.

KEEP IT CLEAN

Most enameled Dutch ovens are dishwasher safe; check the manufacturer's instructions to be sure. Anodized aluminum pots are generally not dishwasher safe; the aluminum will become discolored. Because of their large size, you may prefer to wash Dutch ovens by hand with soap and a sponge or nylon kitchen scrubbie. Don't use anything abrasive like steel wool, as it can scratch the coating. For most stuck-on food, filling the pot with about an inch of hot water and letting it sit for 10 minutes will loosen the sticky bits so they can easily be scrubbed off or washed off in the dishwasher. For serious sticking, a product called Barkeeper's Friend is my go-to cleaner. Just be sure to rinse thoroughly within one minute of application and then dry (if it dries on the surface, it can dull the enamel). I also use the product occasionally when the enamel gets discolored or sticky. Le Creuset and a few other manufacturers also make enamel cleaners that will keep your enamel looking its best.

MAKING THE MOST OF YOUR LEFTOVERS

A Dutch oven can be ideal for making large batches of stews, soups, and braises with leftovers in mind. In fact, many of the recipes in this book taste great when reheated. Much as I love my Dutch oven for this kind of cooking, I never store leftover food in the cooking pot. The heat retention that makes it so wonderful to cook with means that it also takes a long time to cool down, and that can make for unsafe food and an over-worked refrigerator. Instead, transfer the food to a container with an airtight lid, or to a bowl covered with plastic wrap, and let cool on the counter to room temperature before moving it to the refrigerator.

If you're the kind of cook who likes to get creative with leftovers, a Dutch oven can provide ample opportunity for improvising. You can cook a batch of chickpeas on the weekend, for instance, then use some in a salad for lunches, use another portion in a soup, and puree the rest into hummus for a delicious snack later in the week. Or cook a roast for Sunday dinner, then use the remainder of the meat for French dip sandwiches or tacos when you're pressed for time midweek.

A DOABLE FEAST

We all know the feeling: You get home from work or picking up the kids, and you have little time and less energy to devote to making dinner. While I can't make that feeling disappear, I can give you some tips to make your dinner prep easier and more efficient.

- ◆ If you need to thaw meat for dinner, take it out the night before (two nights before for large roasts) and place it in a bowl or rimmed plate on the bottom shelf of the refrigerator. Frozen vegetables thaw quickly, so there's no need to take them out.

- ◆ If you're chopping or slicing sturdy vegetables like onions and bell peppers and you know you'll need them for several meals throughout the week, chop the extra and store them in a plastic bag in the refrigerator for up to two days.

- ◆ If your dinner requires boiling water for pasta or steaming, fill the pot, cover it, and place it over high heat before you start any other prep.

- ◆ Make sure that your Dutch oven and any utensils you'll need for dinner are clean and ready to use.

ABOUT THE RECIPES

All the recipes in this book are designed for a 5.5- to 6.5-quart Dutch oven. Rather than organize the dishes by main ingredient, I've divided them by their recipe style, so to speak. Quick recipes will be found in chapter 2: 30-Minute Meals (page 13), while those with limited ingredients are in chapter 3: Eight-Ingredient Showstoppers (page 31). If you're looking to reduce your cleanup, chapter 4: One-Pot Favorites (page 51) is the place to start. And for those days when you have more time or want a fancier dinner, I've included those recipes in chapter 5: Original Slow Cookers (page 71) and chapter 6: Everyday Decadence (page 87). Although many of the recipes are written to provide a full meal, the final chapter includes side dishes that will complement a wide variety of menus. I've tried as much as possible to provide a wide variety of main ingredients, flavor profiles, and cuisines, so whatever your cooking style and tastes, you'll find plenty of dishes (with nutritional information) to tempt you.

The time necessary to complete the dish is listed at the top of each recipe. "Active" time includes the time for preparing ingredients, finishing the dish, or tasks that require attention during the cooking process. "Total" time amounts to how long a recipe will take to make (from start to finish) so you can gauge what time everyone should start gathering at the table.

Dietary Labels

Because different cooks and their family members can have different dietary needs, I've included a wide variety of recipes that can fit into almost any diet. The recipes are labeled so you can easily tell at a glance whether they'll fit in with your particular preferences:

GLUTEN-FREE: No ingredients contain gluten. If commercial products are called for (for instance, store-bought salsa), those ingredients typically do not contain gluten, but you should check your brands to be sure.

NUT-FREE: No ingredients contain nuts or nut oils.

VEGETARIAN: No ingredients contain meat or meat stock; may include cheese, milk products, or eggs.

DAIRY-FREE: No ingredients contain milk or milk products; may contain eggs.

Helpful Tips

All the recipes are followed by tips to help you get the most from your effort. They'll fall into one of the three following categories:

SERVE IT WITH: Suggestions for accompaniments that will turn the recipe into a full meal. These may be side dishes from chapter 7, or an easy standard, like a green salad or steamed rice.

EASY SUB: Possible substitutions for ingredients that may be difficult to find, out of season, or not to your liking. If there's an easy way to adapt a recipe for a dietary restriction, you'll find that here as well.

HELPFUL HINT: Extra information on a technique that may be unusual, a method for making the recipe easier, or potential mistakes to avoid.

Scaling Recipes

The recipes in this book are mostly written for four servings; some yield six servings. But what if you want to double them for company or for leftovers? Or what if you only want two servings? It's not difficult, but there are a few tricks to keep in mind. First, it's best not to scale up or down by a factor of more than two (that is, doubling or halving a recipe). More drastic scaling can lead to trouble.

For most ingredients, multiply or divide by two. But there are exceptions (of course!):

- If oil or butter is used for searing meat or sweating vegetables, don't change the amount of oil. You want enough fat to coat the pot, and that won't change if you're browning one pound of chicken or two.
- For a liquid that's used to deglaze a pan (usually wine), you can increase or decrease the amount—but not by much. That's because you need a certain amount to get the browned bits off the bottom before reducing.
- When braising, don't automatically double or halve the liquid ingredients. Use just enough liquid to partially submerge the meat.

Finally, in most cases, as long as the ingredients are cut the same, the cooking times generally won't change. The exception is for large pieces of meat—if you use a 4-pound roast instead of a 2-pound roast, the cooking time will obviously increase. But it probably won't double; you'll want to keep an eye on it and let temperature or tenderness be your guide.

EASY BUTTER CHICKEN (PAGE 24)

CHAPTER TWO

30-Minute Meals

When time is short, you might not immediately think of your Dutch oven. But it can turn out a multitude of meals quickly, from stir-fries to pasta to quick stews. All the recipes in this chapter can be finished in 30 minutes, and many of them are complete meals, making dinner even easier. The key with these recipes is prepping some ingredients while others cook so you can make the most of your time.

HUNAN CHICKEN and ASPARAGUS

DAIRY-FREE

ACTIVE TIME: 25 minutes
TOTAL TIME: 25 minutes

Chiles and vinegar give Hunan dishes their characteristic tangy heat. This recipe pairs crunchy fried chicken nuggets with crisp asparagus in a light, savory sauce. Serve over steamed rice, or alone for a low-carb option. SERVES 4

1 pound boneless skinless chicken thighs

1 teaspoon kosher salt

2 cups, plus 1 tablespoon vegetable oil, divided

½ cup, plus 1 teaspoon cornstarch, divided

2 tablespoons low-sodium chicken stock

2 tablespoons soy sauce

2 tablespoons rice vinegar

2 tablespoons Asian chili-garlic sauce

1 tablespoon sesame oil

1 pound asparagus, cut into 1-inch pieces

4 scallions, both white and green parts, sliced and divided

2 garlic cloves, minced

1 teaspoon minced fresh ginger

¼ cup coarsely chopped roasted salted peanuts

1. Sprinkle the chicken with the salt.

2. In a Dutch oven, heat 2 cups of the oil over medium-high heat until it shimmers. While it heats, cut the chicken into 1-inch pieces and toss in a bowl with ½ cup of the cornstarch.

3. Add the chicken to the oil and cook for 3 to 5 minutes, stirring, or until golden brown. Using a slotted spoon or spider, transfer to a rack. Empty the oil from the pot.

4. Add the remaining 1 tablespoon oil to the pot and heat over medium-high heat until shimmering. While the oil heats, in a small bowl, whisk together the chicken stock, soy sauce, vinegar, chili-garlic sauce, sesame oil, and the remaining teaspoon of cornstarch.

5. Add the asparagus, scallion whites, garlic, and ginger to the pot. Cook for 3 to 5 minutes, stirring, until the asparagus is browned in spots and tender. Pour in the sauce and cook for about 1 minute, until thickened. Add the chicken and stir to coat with the sauce.

6. Garnish with scallion greens and peanuts.

EASY SUB: If asparagus isn't in season, green beans also work well in this dish.

PER SERVING: Calories: 366; Total fat: 27g; Carbohydrates: 14g; Fiber: 2.5g; Protein: 18g; Sodium: 1,102mg

SPICY ORANGE BEEF and BROCCOLI

ACTIVE TIME: 20 minutes

TOTAL TIME: 25 minutes

My take on the Chinese American classic, this dish combines steak and broccoli in a light sauce bright with citrus flavor yet deep and complex from the oyster sauce. SERVES 4

2 tablespoons vegetable oil, divided

1 pound sirloin or flat iron steak

1 teaspoon kosher salt, divided

3 cups broccoli florets

3 garlic cloves, minced or pressed

½ teaspoon red pepper flakes

½ cup orange juice, divided

¼ cup low-sodium chicken stock

3 tablespoons dry sherry

¼ cup oyster sauce

1. In a Dutch oven, heat 1 tablespoon of the oil over medium heat until it shimmers. While it heats, sprinkle the steak with ¾ teaspoon of the salt. Sear the steak for 4 minutes on each side, until browned, then remove and set aside.

2. Heat the remaining 1 tablespoon of oil until shimmering. Add the broccoli, garlic, red pepper flakes, and remaining ¼ teaspoon of salt, and stir. Add ¼ cup of the orange juice and the chicken stock and cover. Cook for 4 minutes, until barely tender.

3. While the broccoli cooks, cut the steak into ¼-inch-thick slices.

4. Remove the lid. Add the sherry and stir until it's mostly evaporated. Add the oyster sauce, remaining ¼ cup orange juice, and steak. Stir to coat with the sauce and let sit several minutes to finish cooking the meat.

SERVE IT WITH: Serve over rice or noodles, if desired.

PER SERVING: Calories: 257: Total fat: 12g: Carbohydrates: 9g; Fiber: 1.5g: Protein: 29g: Sodium: 866mg

SLOPPY JOES

ACTIVE TIME: 10 minutes
TOTAL TIME: 30 minutes

When in the mood for a childhood favorite, Sloppy Joes are a great choice. My version is complex and savory, but not too spicy. If you like it hot, add ½ teaspoon of Tabasco or a pinch of cayenne. **SERVES 4**

1 pound ground beef

1 small onion, chopped

½ small red or green
  bell pepper, seeded
  and chopped

1 garlic clove, minced
  or pressed

1 teaspoon kosher salt

1 cup tomato sauce

2 tablespoons cider or
  wine vinegar

2 tablespoons brown sugar

1 tablespoon
  Dijon-style mustard

1 teaspoon
  Worcestershire sauce

4 hamburger buns

1. Place the Dutch oven over medium heat and cook the ground beef for 2 to 3 minutes, stirring to break it up. When the beef is brown, add the onion, bell pepper, and garlic. Season with the salt and continue to cook for about 4 minutes, until the beef is browned and any water has evaporated. Blot off any fat in the pot.

2. Turn the heat to medium-low. Add the tomato sauce, vinegar, sugar, mustard, and Worcestershire sauce. Stir to combine, scraping up the browned bits from the bottom of the pot. Bring to a simmer and cover.

3. Cook for 20 minutes and check the mixture. It should be thick enough that a spoonful mostly holds shape. As necessary, simmer for a few minutes with the lid off so it thickens.

4. Let cool slightly and serve on the hamburger buns.

SERVE IT WITH: Crispy Onion Rings (page 111) and a green salad turn the sandwiches into an extra-satisfying meal.

PER SERVING: Calories: 431; Total fat: 19g; Carbohydrates: 36g; Fiber: 2g; Protein: 28g; Sodium: 1,001mg

NEXT-DAY FRIED RICE

DAIRY-FREE | **NUT-FREE** | **VEGETARIAN**

ACTIVE TIME: 25 minutes
TOTAL TIME: 25 minutes

Fried rice is the perfect way to use up leftover rice, since it has a chance to dry out slightly, meaning it will absorb the sauce for tasty results. You'll have the best results if the rice is at room temperature. SERVES 4

2 tablespoons, plus
  2 teaspoons vegetable
  oil, divided
⅔ cup sliced cremini
  mushrooms
1 tablespoon minced garlic
1 tablespoon
  minced ginger
3 scallions, both green and
  white parts, diced
½ large red bell pepper,
  seeded and diced
3 cups cooked rice, cooled
½ cup frozen peas, thawed
2 eggs, beaten
3 tablespoons soy sauce
1 tablespoon rice vinegar
2 teaspoons toasted
  sesame oil
1 teaspoon Asian chili
  sauce or Sriracha sauce

1. In a Dutch oven, heat 2 tablespoons of the oil over medium-high heat until shimmering. Add the mushrooms and sauté for 4 to 5 minutes, until lightly browned. Add the garlic and ginger and cook, stirring, for 1 minute. Add the scallions and bell pepper and cook, stirring, for 2 to 3 minutes. Add the rice and cook for 2 to 3 minutes, stirring. Stir in the peas.

2. Reduce the heat to medium. Move the rice and vegetables to the perimeter of the pot. Add the remaining 2 teaspoons of oil to the middle and heat until shimmering. Add the eggs and stir to scramble for about 1 minute, breaking them up into medium-size curds before stirring them into the rice and vegetables.

3. Add the soy sauce, vinegar, sesame oil, and chili sauce and toss to coat.

HELPFUL HINT: To save time, look for frozen cubes of minced ginger and garlic (Dorot is the brand I use). Pastes in tubes and jars tend to have less flavor than frozen.

PER SERVING: Calories: 314; Total fat: 14g; Carbohydrates: 38g; Fiber: 1g; Protein: 8g; Sodium: 936mg

CHICKEN and WHITE BEAN CHILI

GLUTEN-FREE | NUT-FREE

ACTIVE TIME: 15 minutes
TOTAL TIME: 30 minutes

Canned beans and chiles cut way down on the cooking time for this Southwestern stew, making it a great way to satisfy your chili craving without spending all day at the stove. **SERVES 4**

2 tablespoons
   vegetable oil
⅔ cup corn kernels
½ small onion, chopped
1 jalapeño, seeded
   and minced
1 teaspoon kosher
   salt, divided
1 cup low-sodium
   chicken stock
1 tablespoon chili powder
1 teaspoon ground cumin
¼ teaspoon ground
   cayenne
1 pound boneless skinless
   chicken breast, cut into
   1-inch cubes
2 (15-ounce) cans
   cannellini beans, drained
1 (4-ounce) can diced
   green chiles
¼ cup sour cream
¼ cup chopped fresh
   cilantro leaves

1. In a Dutch oven, heat the oil over medium-high heat until shimmering. Add the corn in a single layer and let cook without stirring for 3 to 4 minutes, until the corn starts to char.

2. Add the onion, jalapeño, and ¼ teaspoon of the salt and cook for 2 to 3 minutes, stirring, until the onions start to brown.

3. Add the chicken stock and stir, scraping the bottom of the pot to get up any browned bits.

4. Stir in the chili powder, cumin, remaining ¾ teaspoon of salt, and cayenne. Bring to a simmer over medium-low heat and add the chicken, beans, and green chiles and their juices. Cover and cook for 15 minutes, or until the chicken is cooked through.

5. Ladle into bowls and garnish with sour cream and cilantro.

HELPFUL HINT: While charring the corn adds great flavor, you can skip that step and just add it with the chicken and beans for an even faster meal.

PER SERVING: Calories: 458; Total fat: 13g; Carbohydrates: 43g; Fiber: 11g; Protein: 42g; Sodium: 1,122mg

PASTA NIÇOISE

DAIRY-FREE | NUT-FREE

ACTIVE TIME: 20 minutes
TOTAL TIME: 30 minutes

In this pasta version of salade Niçoise, anchovies and tomatoes melt into wine and olive oil to form a light but savory sauce for the pasta, tuna, and beans. It's a fresh, delicious taste of the Mediterranean that will brighten up any weeknight.

SERVES 4

1 tablespoon kosher salt

6 ounces green beans

12 ounces farfalle, rotini, or penne

2 cups cherry tomatoes, divided

¼ cup olive oil

2 garlic cloves, minced or pressed

2 teaspoons anchovy paste

⅔ cup dry white wine

2 (5-ounce) cans oil-packed tuna, drained

½ cup pitted Kalamata olives

¼ teaspoon black pepper

¼ teaspoon red pepper flakes

1. In a Dutch oven, bring 2 quarts of water and the salt to a boil over high.

2. Meanwhile, cut the green beans in half.

3. Once the water is boiling, add the pasta and cook according to package directions. Four minutes before the pasta is done, add the green beans.

4. While the pasta and green beans cook, cut the tomatoes in half.

5. When the pasta is al dente, remove 1 cup of the cooking water and set it aside. Drain the pasta and green beans in a colander.

6. In the Dutch oven, heat the oil over medium heat until shimmering. Add 1 cup of the tomatoes, garlic, and anchovy paste. Cook for about 3 minutes, stirring, until the tomatoes have collapsed. Add the wine and cook until reduced by half.

7. Add the pasta, green beans, tuna, remaining 1 cup of tomatoes, olives, black pepper, and red pepper flakes to the pot. Stir gently to combine. Cook for 2 to 3 minutes or until warmed through. Add reserved pasta water as necessary to loosen the sauce.

HELPFUL HINT: Since the pasta and green beans will cook again, it's best to boil only until the pasta is al dente.

PER SERVING: Calories: 644; Total fat: 24g; Carbohydrates: 73g; Fiber: 5.5g; Protein: 27g; Sodium: 799mg

FISH FILLET SANDWICHES

ACTIVE TIME: 30 minutes
TOTAL TIME: 30 minutes

Crispy fish sandwiches with lemon-pepper aioli from scratch on a weeknight? The trick is to heat the oil slowly while you do all the prep. With tangy coleslaw on the side, you've got dinner. SERVES 4

4 cups vegetable oil

4 (4-ounce) cod or grouper fillets

1 teaspoon kosher salt, divided

½ cup, plus 1 tablespoon rice flour or cornstarch, divided

2 teaspoons lemon juice

¼ teaspoon minced garlic

¾ cup mayonnaise

½ teaspoon coarse-ground black pepper

½ cup all-purpose flour

½ teaspoon baking powder

½ cup vodka

½ cup beer

4 hamburger buns

8 lettuce leaves

1 medium cucumber, sliced

1. In a Dutch oven, heat the oil over medium-low heat to 360°F.

2. Season the fish with ½ teaspoon of the salt. Dust lightly with 1 tablespoon of the rice flour.

3. In a small bowl, whisk together the lemon juice and garlic. Let sit for a minute, then stir in the mayonnaise and pepper. Set aside.

4. In a separate bowl, whisk together the remaining ½ cup of rice flour, all-purpose flour, remaining ½ teaspoon salt, and baking powder. When the oil is hot, stir in the vodka and beer to make a smooth batter.

5. Dip the fillets into the batter and place in the oil. Cook for 4 to 5 minutes, turning once, until golden brown. Place on a rack to drain.

6. Spread the bottom halves of the buns with aioli. Place a fillet, lettuce, and cucumber on each bottom bun. Top with a dollop of aioli and the other half of the bun.

HELPFUL HINT: You may want to cut the fillets in half and fry in batches, so as not to crowd the pot. Just place the first batch on a rack over a sheet pan in a low oven to keep warm.

PER SERVING: Calories: 733; Total fat: 47g; Carbohydrates: 44g; Fiber: 2g; Protein: 25g; Sodium: 768mg

STEAMED HALIBUT with SPINACH and CARROTS

GLUTEN-FREE | **NUT-FREE**

ACTIVE TIME: 13 minutes
TOTAL TIME: 30 minutes

Mustard and dill are one of my favorite flavor complements for halibut. When it's served over a bed of savory spinach and carrots, it becomes an elegant low-carb dinner. SERVES 4

¼ cup (½ stick) unsalted butter, at room temperature, divided

4 tablespoons chopped fresh dill, divided

1 tablespoon Dijon mustard

4 (5-ounce) halibut fillets

2 teaspoons kosher salt, divided

3 carrots, thinly sliced

2 pounds fresh spinach

1. In a small bowl, mix together 2 tablespoons of the butter, 1 tablespoon of the dill, and the mustard. Set aside.

2. Sprinkle the fish with 1 teaspoon of the salt.

3. In a Dutch oven, melt the remaining 2 tablespoons of butter over medium-high heat, until foaming. Add the carrots and the remaining 1 teaspoon of salt and cook for 1 minute, until the carrots start to soften. Add the spinach a couple of handfuls at a time and cook, stirring, until the spinach wilts. Continue adding all the spinach, then stir in the remaining 3 tablespoons of dill.

4. Place the fillets on top of the spinach and spread with the dill butter.

5. Cover the pot and steam for 15 to 18 minutes, or until the fish flakes apart.

EASY SUB: Salmon is a wonderful substitute for the halibut. Depending on the thickness of the fillets, it may cook more quickly than halibut.

PER SERVING: Calories: 307; Total fat: 14g; Carbohydrates: 12g; Fiber: 6.5g; Protein: 32g; Sodium: 959mg

THAI MIXED VEGETABLE CURRY

DAIRY-FREE | GLUTEN-FREE | VEGETARIAN

ACTIVE TIME: 10 minutes
TOTAL TIME: 30 minutes

When I'm in a hurry without a plan for dinner, curry paste and coconut milk are my saviors. Just about any protein and vegetables can be simmered in this fragrant sauce for a quick, delicious meal. **SERVES 4**

1 tablespoon vegetable oil

1 tablespoon Thai red curry paste

1 (13.5-ounce) can full-fat coconut milk

2 cups cauliflower florets

1 large sweet potato, peeled and cut into 1-inch chunks

1 small green bell pepper, seeded and cut into 1-inch chunks

1 small onion, sliced

¾ cup frozen peas, thawed

⅓ cup roasted salted cashews

2 tablespoons coarsely chopped basil

1. In a Dutch oven, heat the oil over medium heat until shimmering. Add the curry paste and stir it into the oil for 1 to 2 minutes, or until fragrant.

2. Add the coconut milk and bring to a simmer.

3. Add the cauliflower, sweet potato, pepper, and onion and stir to combine. Cover the pot and reduce to medium-low heat. Simmer for 16 to 18 minutes, or until the vegetables are tender. Stir in the peas and cook for another minute.

4. Serve over rice, if desired, garnished with the cashews and basil.

EASY SUB: Some commercial Thai curry pastes contain fish sauce or dried shrimp. For a completely vegetarian version, be sure to look for a brand that does not.

PER SERVING: Calories: 254; Total fat: 16g; Carbohydrates: 22g; Fiber: 4.5g; Protein: 6g; Sodium: 398mg

EASY BUTTER CHICKEN

GLUTEN-FREE | **NUT-FREE**

ACTIVE TIME: 20 minutes
TOTAL TIME: 30 minutes

One of India's most popular culinary exports, butter chicken was supposedly invented by a restaurateur to use leftover tandoori chicken. Whatever its origin, this dish of tender chicken in a rich, creamy sauce is sure to please. **SERVES 6**

2 pounds boneless, skinless chicken thighs

2 teaspoons kosher salt, divided

4 tablespoons (½ stick) unsalted butter, divided

1 small onion, chopped

3 garlic cloves, minced

1 teaspoon minced fresh ginger

1 small cinnamon stick (optional)

2 teaspoons garam masala, divided

1 teaspoon ground cumin

½ teaspoon ground turmeric

1 (14.5-ounce) can diced tomatoes

¼ cup water

1 teaspoon smoked paprika

½ cup heavy cream

¼ cup sliced scallions, green part only

¼ cup fresh cilantro or small basil leaves

1. Salt the chicken on both sides with 1 teaspoon of salt.

2. In a Dutch oven, melt 2 tablespoons of butter over medium-high heat, until foaming. Add the onion and cook for 3 minutes, stirring, until softened.

3. Add the garlic, ginger, cinnamon stick (if using), 1 teaspoon of garam masala, cumin, and turmeric. Cook for 1 to 2 minutes, until fragrant.

4. Add the tomatoes and their juices, water, and the remaining 1 teaspoon of salt. Stir to combine and bring to a simmer, uncovered, for 6 minutes.

5. While the sauce cooks, cut the chicken into 1-inch pieces.

6. Using a large fork or potato masher, crush the tomato mixture to make a coarse puree. Add the chicken pieces to the sauce and cook, covered, for 10 minutes. Halfway through, stir in the remaining 1 teaspoon of garam masala and the paprika.

7. Uncover the pot and stir in the remaining 2 tablespoons of butter and cream. Simmer for 5 minutes. Garnish with scallions and cilantro.

SERVE IT WITH: Steamed rice with broccoli or green beans on the side pair well with this dish.

PER SERVING: Calories: 326; Total fat: 20g; Carbohydrates: 6g; Fiber: 1g; Protein: 32g; Sodium: 666mg

PEANUT-SESAME NOODLES with PORK and CUCUMBERS

ACTIVE TIME: 20 minutes
TOTAL TIME: 30 minutes

Spicy pork and cool cucumbers mix with saucy noodles in this Asian-inspired meal. English cucumbers have thinner skin than regular cucumbers and don't need to be peeled. SERVES 4

1 tablespoon kosher salt

3 tablespoons soy sauce

2 tablespoons peanut butter

6 teaspoons toasted sesame oil, divided

1 tablespoon rice vinegar

1 teaspoon red pepper flakes

½ English cucumber

8 ounces Chinese wheat noodles

1 tablespoon vegetable oil

1 pound ground pork

2 teaspoons minced fresh ginger

2 teaspoons minced garlic

⅓ cup coarsely chopped roasted salted peanuts

2 scallions, both white and green parts, sliced

1. In a Dutch oven, bring 2 quarts of water and the salt to a boil over high heat.

2. Meanwhile, in a small bowl, stir together the soy sauce, peanut butter, 4 teaspoons of sesame oil, rice vinegar, and red pepper flakes. Cut the cucumber into ¼-inch-thick slices and cut the slices in half.

3. Add the noodles to the boiling water and cook, stirring, according to package directions. When done, pour into a colander. Rinse with cool water and let drain. Toss with the remaining 2 teaspoons of sesame oil.

4. Wipe the Dutch oven dry and heat the vegetable oil over medium heat until shimmering.

5. Add the pork and cook for 3 to 4 minutes, stirring to break up. When it's no longer pink, add the ginger and garlic and continue to cook until the pork is browned. Add the noodles and sauce and stir to coat, then stir in the cucumbers.

6. Top with the peanuts and scallions.

EASY SUB: I use KAME brand Chinese noodles for this dish, but if you can't find them, you can substitute 2 packages of ramen noodles without the seasoning.

PER SERVING: Calories: 695; Total fat: 44g; Carbohydrates: 46g; Fiber: 2.5g; Protein: 29g; Sodium: 1,270mg

PORK PICCATA

NUT-FREE

ACTIVE TIME: 30 minutes
TOTAL TIME: 30 minutes

Tender pork slices are browned in butter, then topped with a tangy sauce with capers and parsley, for an elegant weeknight entrée. Flattening the pork slices ensures quick, even cooking. SERVES 4

1 (1¼-pound)
   pork tenderloin
1½ teaspoons kosher
   salt, divided
½ cup flour
6 tablespoons (¾ stick)
   unsalted butter, divided
¼ cup lemon juice
¼ cup low-sodium
   chicken stock
3 tablespoons capers
3 tablespoons chopped
   fresh parsley

1. Slice the pork into 1½-inch-thick medallions. Cover the pork slices with a piece of plastic wrap and use a mallet or small skillet to flatten the medallions to about ¼ inch. Season on both sides with 1 teaspoon of the salt, then dredge lightly in the flour.

2. In a Dutch oven, heat 2 tablespoons of the butter over medium heat until foaming. Add half the pork and cook for 3 to 4 minutes, until deep golden brown. Turn the slices and cook on the other side for another 3 minutes, or until browned. Transfer the pork to a plate or a rack. Repeat with 2 tablespoons of the butter and the remaining pork.

3. Add the lemon juice, chicken stock, and capers to the pot over medium-high heat. Bring the liquid to a boil, scraping up any browned bits, and cook until reduced by about half.

4. Remove the Dutch oven from the burner and let cool for 1 to 2 minutes. One tablespoon at a time, swirl in the remaining 2 tablespoons of butter to thicken the sauce slightly. Stir in the parsley. Add the pork medallions and turn over to coat with the sauce and reheat.

SERVE IT WITH: Buttered noodles and steamed green beans or Green Beans Amandine (page 107) are a good match.

PER SERVING: Calories: 329; Total fat: 21g; Carbohydrates: 5g; Fiber: 0.5g; Protein: 29g; Sodium: 992mg

MUSSELS in GARLIC WINE SAUCE

GLUTEN-FREE | NUT-FREE

ACTIVE TIME: 10 minutes

TOTAL TIME: 15 minutes

If you've never cooked mussels at home, you owe it to yourself to give this recipe a try. Within a few minutes, you'll get a wildly flavorful sauce for the plump bivalves. SERVES 4

2 pounds mussels,
   debearded and cleaned

4 tablespoons (½ stick)
   unsalted butter, divided

1 shallot, minced

3 garlic cloves, minced

¾ cup dry white wine

½ cup clam juice

3 tablespoons chopped
   fresh chives

1. Sort through the mussels, discarding any that don't close when tapped.

2. In a Dutch oven, heat 2 tablespoons of the butter over medium-high heat. Add the shallot and garlic and cook for 1 to 2 minutes, or until fragrant. Add the wine and clam juice, and bring to a boil. Add the mussels and cover the pot.

3. Steam for 3 to 4 minutes, or until the mussels have opened. Transfer the mussels to a large bowl, leaving the liquid behind. Cut the remaining 2 tablespoons of butter into 4 pieces and stir in one piece at a time. Stir in the chives and pour the liquid over the mussels.

SERVE IT WITH: Crusty bread for dipping and a green salad make a lovely light meal.

PER SERVING: Calories: 348; Total fat: 16g; Carbohydrates: 12g; Fiber: 0.5g; Protein: 28g; Sodium: 792mg

SMOKED SALMON and CORN CHOWDER

ACTIVE TIME: 10 minutes
TOTAL TIME: 30 minutes

Smoked salmon is a wonderful match for corn, and this recipe combines the two in a quick, delicious chowder. For a slightly thicker texture, substitute russet potatoes for the Yukon Golds; the starch in russets dissolves more readily into the soup. SERVES 4

2 tablespoons
   unsalted butter
1 small leek, white
   and light green parts
   only, chopped
1 teaspoon kosher salt
1 tablespoon
   all-purpose flour
¼ cup dry white wine
3 cups whole milk
1 cup half-and-half
1 medium Yukon Gold
   potato, peeled and cut
   into ½-inch cubes
1½ cups corn kernels
6 ounces hot-smoked
   salmon, chopped
1 teaspoon grated
   lemon zest

1. In a Dutch oven, melt the butter over medium heat until foaming. Add the leek and sprinkle with the salt. Cook for 1 to 2 minutes, or until softened. Stir in the flour and cook for 1 to 2 minutes, or until light tan.

2. Add the wine and stir to combine.

3. Add the milk and half-and-half, and bring to a simmer.

4. Add the potato and corn and cook, partially covered, for 15 minutes, or until the potato is tender.

5. Add the salmon and lemon zest and stir to heat through.

EASY SUB: If you can't find leeks, substitute chopped onion or scallions.

PER SERVING: Calories: 380; Total fat: 21g; Carbohydrates: 30g; Fiber: 2g; Protein: 18g; Sodium: 817mg

COTTAGE PIE

NUT-FREE

ACTIVE TIME: 10 minutes
TOTAL TIME: 30 minutes

Cottage pie, like its cousin shepherd's pie, is an easy and delicious way to use up leftovers. Make a double batch of Silky Garlic Mashed Potatoes (page 109) on the weekend and use leftover Garlic Pot Roast with Mushrooms (page 57), and with a quick gravy and frozen vegetables, you have a fast weeknight dinner. SERVES 4

¼ cup (½ stick)
   unsalted butter

1 small onion, chopped

1 teaspoon kosher salt

1 cup frozen mixed
   vegetables, thawed

⅓ cup all-purpose flour

2 cups low-sodium
   beef broth

1 tablespoon
   Worcestershire sauce

1 teaspoon dried thyme

2 cups shredded or
   chopped cooked beef

½ teaspoon black pepper

1 recipe Silky Garlic
   Mashed Potatoes
   (page 109), at
   room temperature

1. Preheat the oven to 400°F.

2. In a Dutch oven, melt the butter over medium heat until foaming. Add the onion and sprinkle with the salt. Cook for 1 to 2 minutes, or until softened. Stir in the vegetables and cook for 1 to 2 minutes, or until their moisture has evaporated.

3. Stir in the flour and cook for 2 to 3 minutes, until light tan.

4. Add the broth and stir to combine. Bring to a simmer and cook for 2 to 3 minutes, or until thickened.

5. Stir in the Worcestershire sauce and thyme.

6. Stir in the beef and black pepper. Spread the mashed potatoes over the mixture.

7. Bake for 15 minutes. Switch the oven to broil and cook for another 5 minutes, or until the potatoes are lightly browned.

EASY SWAP: You can use any cooked meat for this (lamb would turn it into shepherd's pie), and if you don't have leftover mashed potatoes, store-bought potatoes work fine (you'll need about 3 cups).

PER SERVING: Calories: 806; Total fat: 49g; Carbohydrates: 59g; Fiber: 4.5g; Protein: 35g; Sodium: 840mg

SPINACH AND MUSHROOM FETTUCCINE (PAGE 42)

CHAPTER THREE

Eight-Ingredient Showstoppers

Even if your cupboards and fridge aren't teeming with groceries, delicious dinners are still possible. In this chapter, the recipes require five or fewer main ingredients that come together with the simple kitchen staples of kosher salt, freshly ground black pepper, and cooking oil. The key in these recipes is using at least one really flavorful ingredient—jarred pesto, spicy sausage, sharp cheese, or marinara—and it pays to splurge a little on the best versions you can find.

FAJITA-STYLE CHICKEN and RICE

ACTIVE TIME: 15 minutes
TOTAL TIME: 35 minutes

If you cross chicken fajitas with arroz con pollo, you'll get this delicious, easy dinner. The salsa is key to the flavor of the rice, so choose a good one (I like Frontera brand). **SERVES 4**

1½ pounds boneless, skinless chicken thighs, cut into 1-inch strips

2 teaspoons kosher salt, divided

1 tablespoon vegetable oil

1 large red or green bell pepper, seeded and sliced

1 tablespoon ground chili powder

1½ cups long-grain white rice

¾ cup red or green salsa

1. Sprinkle the chicken pieces with ¾ teaspoon of the salt and set aside.

2. In a Dutch oven, heat the oil over medium heat until it shimmers. Add the pepper and cook, stirring, for a few minutes until it begins to soften.

3. Add the chicken and chili powder and stir to distribute the seasoning.

4. Add the rice, salsa, remaining 1¼ teaspoons of salt, and ¾ cup of water to the pot and stir. Over medium heat, bring to a simmer.

5. Cover the pot and reduce the heat to medium-low. Cook for 20 minutes, then remove the lid and gently stir the rice. It should be tender, with no liquid remaining in the pot.

HELPFUL HINT: Try to find a chili powder without salt; otherwise, reduce the salt in the rice to ½ teaspoon.

PER SERVING: Calories: 508; Total fat: 8g; Carbohydrates: 65g; Fiber: 2.5g; Protein: 41g; Sodium: 1,052mg

PIZZA CHICKEN

GLUTEN-FREE NUT-FREE

ACTIVE TIME: 15 minutes

TOTAL TIME: 35 minutes

In the mood for pizza? This fun, easy chicken dinner is better than pepperoni pizza and faster than delivery. I prefer pepperoni that's not sliced thin; a thicker cut adds texture to the sauce. SERVES 4

1 teaspoon kosher salt

1 pound boneless, skinless chicken breast, cut into ¾-inch thick slices

2 tablespoons olive oil

1 cup sliced mushrooms

2½ cups marinara sauce

¾ cup chopped pepperoni

1 cup shredded part-skim mozzarella cheese

1. Preheat the oven to 350°F.

2. Sprinkle the salt on the chicken breast slices. Set aside.

3. In a Dutch oven, heat the oil over medium-high heat. When it shimmers, add the mushrooms. Cook for 5 to 6 minutes, stirring occasionally, until mostly browned.

4. Add the marinara sauce and pepperoni and stir. Bring to a simmer.

5. Place the chicken on top and spoon sauce over to cover. Top with the cheese.

6. Place the Dutch oven, uncovered, in the oven. Cook for 20 minutes, or until the chicken registers 165°F on a meat thermometer and the juices run clear.

SERVE IT WITH: A tossed green salad and garlic bread make the chicken a meal.

PER SERVING: Calories: 467; Total fat: 27g; Carbohydrates: 15g; Fiber: 3g; Protein: 39g; Sodium: 1,586mg

PORK MEDALLIONS and APPLES with MUSTARD SAUCE

ACTIVE TIME: 20 minutes
TOTAL TIME: 35 minutes

Pork tenderloin medallions cook quickly, and the sauce in this recipe is a snap, so you can indulge in this elegant entrée on the busiest of weeknights. The pork is delicious over Silky Garlic Mashed Potatoes (page 109). SERVES 4

1 (1¼-pound)
   pork tenderloin
2 teaspoons kosher
   salt, divided
½ teaspoon black
   pepper, divided
3 tablespoons vegetable
   oil, divided
1 tart apple, peeled,
   cored, and sliced
⅔ cup hard apple cider
½ cup heavy cream
1 tablespoon
   Dijon mustard

PER SERVING: Calories: 392;
Total fat: 25g; Carbohydrates:
9g; Fiber: 1g; Protein: 29g;
Sodium: 1,073mg

1. Slice the pork into medallions about 1½ inches thick. With the palm of your hand, flatten them to about ¾ inch. Season with 1 teaspoon of the salt and ¼ teaspoon of the black pepper.

2. In a Dutch oven, heat 1 tablespoon of the oil over medium heat until shimmering. Add half the pork medallions and cook for 3 or 4 minutes, or until deep golden brown. Turn the slices and cook on the other side for 3 minutes, or until browned. Transfer the pork to a plate or a rack. Repeat with another table-spoon of oil and the remaining pork.

3. Heat the remaining 1 tablespoon of oil until shimmer-ing. Add the apple slices and cook for 4 to 5 minutes, stirring occasionally, until browned. Add the cider and cook for 2 to 3 minutes, scraping up the browned bits, until reduced by about half. Stir in the cream and mustard and cook for about 5 minutes, until the sauce has thickened slightly.

4. Return the pork to the pot and turn to coat with the sauce and rewarm. Sprinkle with the remaining ¼ teaspoon of black pepper and 1 teaspoon of salt.

SIMPLE SUB: If you can't find hard cider, use half regular apple cider and half water. Regular cider can be quite sweet, though, so you may want to add a splash of cider vinegar.

ROASTED ITALIAN SAUSAGES with GRAPES

ACTIVE TIME: 15 minutes
TOTAL TIME: 40 minutes

When I first read about cooking Italian sausages with grapes, I was skeptical, but it turns out to be amazingly good. The grapes soften and almost melt into a tangy sauce, which complements the spicy sausages perfectly. SERVES 4

3 tablespoons olive
   oil, divided
6 links (about 1½ pounds)
   hot Italian sausage
2 pounds seedless
   red grapes
3 shallots, sliced
2 teaspoons fresh
   thyme or 1 teaspoon
   dried thyme
½ teaspoon kosher salt
¼ teaspoon black pepper
3 tablespoons
   balsamic vinegar

1. Preheat the oven to 375°F.

2. In a Dutch oven, heat 1 tablespoon of the oil over medium-high heat. When shimmering, add the sausages and brown for 6 to 8 minutes, turning halfway through.

3. While the sausages brown, in a large bowl, combine the grapes, shallots, thyme, salt, and pepper. Drizzle with the remaining 2 tablespoons of oil and toss to coat.

4. When the sausages are browned, add the grape mixture to the Dutch oven, moving the sausages over the mixture.

5. Transfer the pot to the oven, uncovered, and roast for 20 to 25 minutes, or until the grapes are very soft and the sausages are done. Remove the pot from the oven and drizzle the vinegar over, stirring to coat.

SERVE IT WITH: Roasted Red Pepper Polenta (page 112) goes very well with the sausages.

PER SERVING: Calories: 870; Total fat: 57g; Carbohydrates: 50g; Fiber: 2.5g; Protein: 35g; Sodium: 1,411mg

HOISIN-GINGER SHORT RIBS

ACTIVE TIME: 10 minutes

TOTAL TIME: 4 hours 30 minutes

These savory, Asian-inspired short ribs couldn't be easier—after a few minutes of prep time, they cook unattended, filling the kitchen with irresistible aromas, while you're free to do other things. SERVES 4

1½ teaspoons kosher salt

4 pounds bone-in short ribs

½ cup hoisin sauce

1 tablespoon minced ginger

1 teaspoon Asian chili-garlic sauce

1 tablespoon rice vinegar

1. Salt the short ribs on all sides.

2. Pour the hoisin sauce into a Dutch oven. Add the ginger, chili-garlic sauce, and vinegar and stir to combine. Add the short ribs and turn to coat with the sauce, placing them meat-side down.

3. Place the Dutch oven with the lid ajar in the oven. Turn the oven to 200°F and cook for 1 hour.

4. Increase the heat to 250°F and cook for 2 hours. Finally, increase the heat to 300°F and cook for another 60 to 90 minutes, or until the meat is tender and pulling away from the bones.

5. Remove the pot from the oven and take the ribs out. Spoon or blot off the fat from the sauce and whisk in a few tablespoons of water, serving the sauce over the ribs.

SERVE IT WITH: Steamed rice and Green Beans Amandine (page 107) on the side turn the ribs into a full meal.

PER SERVING: Calories: 875; Total fat: 50g; Carbohydrates: 18g; Fiber: 1g; Protein: 89g; Sodium: 1,393mg

CHORIZO-STUFFED PEPPERS

GLUTEN-FREE | NUT-FREE

ACTIVE TIME: 30 minutes
TOTAL TIME: 1 hour 10 minutes

While these spicy stuffed peppers do take a little time, you can make the stuffing ahead of time, or even stuff them in advance for baking later. Southwestern Creamed Corn (page 104) makes a tasty side. SERVES 4

4 large bell peppers,
   any colors
½ teaspoon kosher salt
1 tablespoon vegetable oil
12 ounces Mexican
   chorizo, casings removed
1½ cups cooked white or
   brown rice
¾ cup diced canned
   tomatoes, drained
1½ cups grated Monterey
   Jack cheese, divided

1. Preheat the oven to 375°F.

2. In a Dutch oven, bring 1 inch of water to a boil.

3. Slice ¼ inch off the top of each pepper, reserving the tops. Remove the core and ribs. Remove the stems from the tops and chop the flesh.

4. Place the peppers, cut-side down, in a steamer basket. Once the water is boiling, insert the basket, cover, and steam for 4 minutes. Remove the basket, turn the peppers over, and sprinkle the insides with the salt. Discard the water.

5. In the Dutch oven, heat the oil over medium heat, until shimmering. Cook the chorizo for 4 to 5 minutes, breaking it up, until mostly browned. Add the chopped peppers and cook for 3 to 4 minutes, until the chorizo is cooked.

6. In a large bowl, combine the chorizo mixture, rice, and tomatoes and stir. Stir in 1 cup of the cheese.

7. Spoon the mixture into the peppers, packing tightly and mounding up. Top with the remaining ½ cup of cheese.

8. Place the peppers in the Dutch oven and cover. Bake for 25 minutes.

9. Remove the lid and continue cooking for another 15 minutes, or until the cheese is melted and slightly browned.

HELPFUL HINT: Mexican chorizo is an uncooked spicy pork sausage, sold in casings and in bulk. Don't substitute Spanish chorizo, which is a smoked, cooked sausage.

PER SERVING: Calories: 538; Total fat: 36g; Carbohydrates: 25g; Fiber: 3g; Protein: 26g; Sodium: 1,386mg

CHILE RELLENO CASSEROLE

GLUTEN-FREE | NUT-FREE | VEGETARIAN

ACTIVE TIME: 15 minutes
TOTAL TIME: 45 minutes

I love chiles rellenos, but they're really time-consuming and messy, so I don't make them often. Fortunately, it's possible to get the flavors of chiles rellenos in this easy, delicious casserole. SERVES 4

6 large eggs

1 teaspoon kosher salt

2 tablespoons olive oil

2 cups mild tomato-based salsa, divided

2 (4-ounce) cans whole green chiles, drained and blotted dry, divided

3 cups shredded Monterey Jack cheese, divided

16 to 20 tortilla chips, lightly crushed

1. Preheat the oven to 350°F.

2. In a medium bowl, whisk the eggs and salt until thoroughly blended.

3. In a Dutch oven, heat the oil over medium-high heat. When it shimmers, pour in the eggs. As the eggs set, lift the edges and let the uncooked egg flow to the bottom of the pot. Cook for 3 to 4 minutes, just until set, then remove from heat.

4. To assemble the casserole, spread 1 cup of the salsa over the eggs. Slit the chiles along one side and open them up. Place half the chiles on top of the salsa layer, laying them flat, then evenly cover the chiles with 1½ cups of the cheese. Top with the remaining chiles, then spread the remaining 1 cup of salsa over top. Top with ¾ cup of the cheese. Mix the remaining ¾ cup of cheese with the crushed tortilla chips and layer the top of the casserole with enough of the chips to cover.

5. Bake for 30 to 35 minutes, or until browned and bubbling.

6. Let rest for a couple of minutes, then slice into wedges and serve.

EASY SUB: For a spicier casserole, use pepper Jack cheese.

PER SERVING: Calories: 568; Total fat: 43g; Carbohydrates: 18g; Fiber: 6.5g; Protein: 29g; Sodium: 1,964mg

CREAMY HAM and POTATO GRATIN

GLUTEN-FREE NUT-FREE

ACTIVE TIME: 10 minutes

TOTAL TIME: 45 minutes

Somewhere near the intersection of broccoli-cheddar soup and scalloped potatoes you'll find this savory casserole. While it bakes, make a quick green salad, and dinner is done! SERVES 4

3 cups broccoli florets

1¼ teaspoons kosher salt, divided

2 cups half-and-half

½ teaspoon black pepper

1¼ pounds Yukon Gold potatoes, peeled and cut into ½-inch cubes

2 cups chopped baked ham or deli ham

2 cups shredded aged cheddar cheese, divided

1. In a Dutch oven, bring 1 inch of water to a boil. While the water heats, place the broccoli in a steamer basket. When the water boils, insert the basket, cover the pot, and steam the broccoli for 3 minutes. Remove the steamer basket and sprinkle the broccoli with ¼ teaspoon of salt. Discard the water.

2. In the Dutch oven, heat the half-and-half over medium-low heat. Stir in the remaining 1 teaspoon of salt and the pepper. Add the potatoes and bring to a light simmer. Cook for 6 to 8 minutes, or until tender.

3. Stir in the ham, broccoli, and 1 cup of cheese. Top with the remaining 1 cup of cheese and bake, uncovered, for 25 minutes, or until bubbling.

HELPFUL HINT: If you like a browned top to your casseroles, turn the oven to broil for the last few minutes of the cooking time. A small chunk of cooked ham from the meat section works well in this recipe. If you can't find one, ask the deli clerk to cut ½-inch-thick ham slices instead.

PER SERVING: Calories: 566; Total fat: 34g; Carbohydrates: 33g; Fiber: 3.5g; Protein: 33g; Sodium: 1,539mg

SPINACH and MUSHROOM FETTUCCINE

ACTIVE TIME: 15 minutes
TOTAL TIME: 35 minutes

Mushrooms and spinach have a wonderful affinity, the earthiness of the mushrooms complementing the bitterness of the greens. In this quick dish, garlic flavors the creamy sauce for the vegetables and pasta. SERVES 4

1 tablespoon plus
  1 teaspoon kosher
  salt, divided
12 ounces fettuccine
2 tablespoons olive oil
1 pound sliced
  shiitake mushrooms
3 garlic cloves, minced
1 cup heavy cream
1 pound fresh
  baby spinach

1. In a Dutch oven, combine 3 quarts of water and 1 tablespoon of the salt. Cover the pot and bring to a boil over high heat. When boiling, add the pasta and stir. Cook according to package directions, until al dente. Reserve 1½ cups of the pasta water, then drain in a colander.

2. Return the pot to the stove and heat the oil over medium heat. When it shimmers, add the mushrooms and the remaining 1 teaspoon of salt and cook, stirring, for 6 to 8 minutes, or until browned.

3. Add the garlic and cook for 1 minute, or until fragrant.

4. Pour 1 cup of reserved pasta water over the fettuccine to loosen it, then add it to the pot.

5. Pour in the cream and bring to a boil, stirring thoroughly. Stir in the spinach to wilt, adding additional pasta water, if necessary, to thin the sauce.

EASY SUB: If you can't find shiitake mushrooms, creminis or a "wild" mushroom blend can be used instead.

PER SERVING: Calories: 641; Total fat: 30g; Carbohydrates: 77g; Fiber: 8g; Protein: 19g; Sodium: 490mg

SWEET and SPICY GLAZED SALMON with BOK CHOY

ACTIVE TIME: 10 minutes
TOTAL TIME: 45 minutes

Thai sweet chili sauce is one of my all-time favorite condiments. In this recipe, I use it to glaze salmon, which is baked over a bed of savory bok choy and scallions. SERVES 4

4 (6-ounce) salmon fillets

4 tablespoons soy sauce, divided

1 small head bok choy

2 tablespoons vegetable oil

5 scallions, both white and green parts, sliced and divided

⅓ cup Thai sweet chili sauce

1. Preheat the oven to 375°F.

2. Brush the salmon fillets on both sides with 2 tablespoons of the soy sauce. Cut the bok choy leaves into ribbons and the stems into ¼-inch-thick slices.

3. In a Dutch oven, heat the oil over medium-high heat. When it shimmers, add the bok choy stems and scallion whites and cook, stirring for 3 to 4 minutes, or until beginning to soften.

4. Stir in the bok choy leaves and the remaining 2 tablespoons of soy sauce. Cook for a minute, until beginning to wilt.

5. Place the salmon on top of the vegetables. Brush with about ¼ cup of the chili sauce, drizzling the remaining sauce over the vegetables.

6. Bake for 15 minutes, or until the fish flakes apart with a fork.

SERVE IT WITH: The dish makes a great low-carb dinner as is, but if you like, steamed rice and roasted potatoes are both good complements.

PER SERVING: Calories: 371; Total fat: 15g; Carbohydrates: 15g; Fiber: 2.5g; Protein: 39g; Sodium: 1,627mg

CREAMY PESTO LINGUINE with SHRIMP

ACTIVE TIME: 15 minutes
TOTAL TIME: 30 minutes

Store-bought pesto makes this pasta dinner as easy as it is delicious. Removing the shrimp after sautéing keeps them plump and succulent, so don't skip that step. SERVES 4

4 teaspoons kosher salt

12 ounces linguine

1 tablespoon extra-virgin olive oil

1 pound (size 21/25) shrimp, peeled and deveined

½ cup pesto

½ cup grated Parmesan cheese

3 tablespoons unsalted butter

1. In a Dutch oven, combine 3 quarts of water and the salt. Cover the pot and bring to a boil over high heat. When boiling, add the pasta and stir. Cook according to package directions until al dente. Reserve 2 cups of the pasta water, then drain in a colander.

2. Return the pot to the stove and heat the oil over medium heat. When it shimmers, add the shrimp and cook for 3 to 4 minutes, stirring, until barely done. Remove from the pot.

3. Pour 1 cup of reserved pasta water over the linguine to loosen it, then add it to the pot. Add the remaining 1 cup of cooking water, pesto, Parmesan, and butter to the pot. Over low heat, toss the pasta and stir vigorously to form a light sauce, about 1 minute. Let the pasta sit for 1 minute.

4. Stir in the shrimp and cover the pot to let them heat through. Before serving, toss again to stir in the shrimp.

HELPFUL HINT: Because the sauce is so simple, it pays to start with great-quality ingredients. Pesto bought from the refrigerated section of the store will be more flavorful than the jar on the shelf, and a chunk of Parmesan that you grate will be better than pre-grated.

PER SERVING: Calories: 679; Total fat: 30g; Carbohydrates: 66g; Fiber: 3.5g; Protein: 35g; Sodium: 715mg

"BACON and EGGS" with WHITE BEANS

GLUTEN-FREE

ACTIVE TIME: 15 minutes
TOTAL TIME: 40 minutes

If you're a fan of breakfast for dinner, you'll love this combination of eggs and white beans garnished with pesto and tomatoes. For a Southwestern twist, try it with black beans and green salsa in place of the white beans and pesto.
SERVES 4

1 tablespoon extra-virgin olive oil

8 ounces (about 1 cup) pancetta, diced

2 (15-ounce) cans cannellini beans

4 eggs

½ teaspoon kosher salt

¼ cup pesto

1 large tomato, seeded and diced

1. In a Dutch oven, heat the oil and pancetta over medium-low heat. Cook, stirring occasionally, until the pancetta is crisp. Move half the pancetta to a paper-towel-lined plate.

2. Drain one can of beans and add all the beans and the juices from one can and simmer for 15 minutes. If you like, mash them lightly with a large fork or potato masher.

3. Make 4 indentations in the beans and crack the eggs in. Sprinkle with the salt. Cover the pot and cook until the eggs are set, about 5 minutes for soft yolks or 8 for firmer eggs.

4. Drizzle with the pesto. Sprinkle the reserved pancetta and tomato over the top.

EASY SUB: If you can't find pancetta, thick-sliced bacon makes a fine substitute.

PER SERVING: Calories: 570; Total fat: 33g; Carbohydrates: 38g; Fiber: 11g; Protein: 30g; Sodium: 1,892mg

CHEESE TORTELLINI with
SUN-DRIED TOMATOES

NUT-FREE VEGETARIAN

ACTIVE TIME: 15 minutes
TOTAL TIME: 25 minutes

Reminiscent of *tortellini en brodo*, the savory Italian soup, this hearty dish features sun-dried tomatoes and arugula, with a hint of lemon. SERVES 4

1 tablespoon kosher salt

1 (20-ounce) package
   frozen cheese tortellini

1 lemon

3 tablespoons olive oil

½ cup sun-dried tomato
   puree with garlic

4 packed cups arugula

1 cup grated
   Parmesan cheese

1. In a Dutch oven, combine 3 quarts of water and the salt. Cover and bring to a boil over high heat. When boiling, add the pasta and stir. Cook according to package directions until al dente. Reserve 2 cups pasta water, then drain in a colander.

2. While the water boils and the tortellini cook, grate a teaspoon of zest from the lemon. Cut the lemon in half and juice it. You should have about 2 tablespoons of lemon juice.

3. Return the pot to the stove and heat the oil over medium heat. When it shimmers, stir in the tomato puree. Cook for about 2 minutes, or until fragrant. Add the tortellini, pasta water, lemon juice, and zest. Add the arugula without stirring and cover the pot for a minute until the arugula mostly wilts. Gently stir in the arugula. Ladle into bowls and top with the cheese.

EASY SUB: If you can't find arugula, use baby spinach instead.

PER SERVING: Calories: 627; Total fat: 30g; Carbohydrates: 63g; Fiber: 5g; Protein: 21g; Sodium: 892mg

STEAK HASH with HORSERADISH SAUCE

GLUTEN-FREE | **NUT-FREE**

ACTIVE TIME: 25 minutes
TOTAL TIME: 35 minutes

I'm embarrassed to admit how old I was when I discovered that hash doesn't have to include corned beef. I've come to prefer it with steak, especially when it's topped with a tangy, spicy horseradish sauce. SERVES 4

12 ounces strip steak

2 teaspoons kosher
salt, divided

⅓ cup sour cream

2 tablespoons prepared
horseradish

½ teaspoon black pepper

1 pound russet potatoes,
peeled and cut into
½-inch dice

3 tablespoons vegetable
oil, divided

1 small onion, chopped

1. Sprinkle the steak with 1 teaspoon of the salt.

2. In a small bowl, whisk together the sour cream, horseradish, and black pepper. Set aside.

3. In a Dutch oven, bring 1 inch of water to a boil. While the water heats, place the potatoes in a steamer basket. When the water boils, insert the basket and cover. Steam for 5 to 8 minutes, or until barely tender. Empty the pot and return it to the stove.

4. In the Dutch oven, heat 1 tablespoon of oil over medium-high heat. When it shimmers, add the steak and sear for 3 to 4 minutes per side, then remove from the pot.

5. Add the remaining 2 tablespoons oil and heat until shimmering. Add the potatoes and onion and sprinkle with the remaining 1 teaspoon of salt. Cook for 6 to 8 minutes, stirring occasionally, until the potatoes are lightly browned.

6. While the vegetables cook, cut the steak into ½-inch pieces. When the potatoes are tender, return the steak to the pot, and stir to cook through. Serve topped with the sauce.

EASY SUB: This dish is great—and even easier—made using leftover steak or Garlic Pot Roast with Mushrooms (page 57).

PER SERVING: Calories: 319; Total fat: 16g; Carbohydrates: 23g; Fiber: 2g; Protein: 23g; Sodium: 613mg

HONEY-CHIPOTLE CHICKEN WINGS

DAIRY-FREE | GLUTEN-FREE | NUT-FREE

ACTIVE TIME: 40 minutes

TOTAL TIME: 2 hours

There are two keys to crispy, beautifully browned chicken wings. First, a little baking powder sprinkled over them increases browning. Second, letting them dry before frying will ensure an extra crisp exterior, even after they get tossed in the sweet-hot sauce. SERVES 4

3 pounds chicken wing
   flats and drumettes
1½ teaspoons kosher salt
1½ teaspoons
   baking powder
4 cups vegetable oil
¼ cup honey
⅓ cup Mexican hot sauce
1 chipotle in adobo,
   minced, with sauce to
   equal 2 teaspoons

1. In a large bowl, place the wings and sprinkle with the salt and baking powder, tossing thoroughly to coat. Arrange the chicken wings on a rack placed in a sheet pan and let sit for 1 hour or refrigerate for 4 to 6 hours, uncovered.

2. In a Dutch oven, heat the oil over medium-high heat until the temperature reads 365°F.

3. While the oil heats, in a large bowl, whisk together the honey, hot sauce, and chipotle with sauce. Set aside.

4. When the oil is at temperature, fry about a quarter of the wings for 8 to 10 minutes, or until the skin is crisp and deep golden brown and the meat is tender. Drain on a rack and repeat with the remaining wings in batches, letting the oil heat back up between batches.

5. Add the cooked wings to the bowl with the sauce and toss to coat.

SERVE IT WITH: To turn the wings into dinner, pair them with Smoky Refried Beans (page 108) or Southwestern Creamed Corn (page 104).

PER SERVING: Calories: 557; Total fat: 36g; Carbohydrates: 19g; Fiber: 0g; Protein: 38g; Sodium: 747mg

CHICKEN PAPRIKASH WITH POTATOES (PAGE 58)

CHAPTER FOUR

One-Pot Favorites

One of the greatest advantages to cooking with a Dutch oven is how many one-pot dinners you can make in it. You may need a bowl for mixing or a colander for draining pasta, but other than that, cleanup will be a breeze. Your Dutch oven will go from the stove or oven straight to the dinner table with a complete meal all in one beautiful pot.

CURRY NOODLES with SHRIMP and SNOW PEAS

ACTIVE TIME: 25 minutes
TOTAL TIME: 25 minutes

This is one of my favorite comfort dishes—noodles and shrimp in a spicy broth laced with coconut milk and curry. The fact that it cooks all in one pot and makes a full meal doesn't hurt, either. You'll find the curry paste and fish sauce in your grocery store's international section. SERVES 4

1 tablespoon kosher salt

8 ounces Chinese wheat noodles, ramen, or angel hair pasta

1 tablespoon sesame oil

1 tablespoon vegetable oil

3 garlic cloves, minced

1 tablespoon Thai red curry paste

1 teaspoon curry powder

1 (13.5-ounce) can full-fat coconut milk

1½ cups low-sodium chicken or vegetable stock

2 tablespoons fish sauce

1 tablespoon sugar

1 pound (size 21/25) shrimp, peeled and deveined

8 ounces snow peas, trimmed

¼ cup coarsely chopped fresh cilantro leaves

¼ cup coarsely chopped roasted peanuts

1. In a Dutch oven, combine 3 quarts of water and the salt. Bring to a boil. Add the noodles and cook according to package directions until al dente. Drain and rinse in cold water. Toss with the sesame oil to coat. Set aside.

2. In the Dutch oven, heat the vegetable oil over medium heat. When it shimmers, add the garlic, curry paste, and curry powder and cook for about 1 minute, until fragrant. Add the coconut milk, stock, fish sauce, and sugar. Bring to a simmer. Cook for about 10 minutes.

3. Add the shrimp and snow peas to the pot and cook for 2 to 3 minutes, until the snow peas are tender and the shrimp are opaque.

4. Add the noodles to heat through. Garnish with cilantro and peanuts.

EASY SUB: Rather than the snow peas, try substituting sliced bok choy or spinach. The bok choy will take slightly longer to cook, the spinach slightly less time.

PER SERVING: Calories: 614; Total fat: 27g; Carbohydrates: 54g; Fiber: 3.5g; Protein: 36g; Sodium: 1,448mg

LASAGNA SOUP

NUT-FREE

ACTIVE TIME: 15 minutes
TOTAL TIME: 35 minutes

Want the delicious flavors of lasagna without the bother of making it? Try this hearty soup, with sausage, tomatoes, pasta, and three kinds of cheese. You may never go back to the baked casserole. SERVES 4

1 tablespoon olive oil

1 pound bulk
   Italian sausage

1 red or green bell pepper,
   seeded and chopped

½ onion, chopped

1 garlic clove, minced

1 (28-ounce) can
   crushed tomatoes

3 cups low-sodium
   chicken stock

½ teaspoon kosher salt

8 ounces farfalle (bow
   tie) pasta

2 tablespoons
   chopped parsley

½ teaspoon black pepper

1 cup loosely
   packed shredded
   mozzarella cheese

4 ounces whole-milk
   ricotta cheese, at
   room temperature

¼ cup grated
   Parmesan cheese

1. In a Dutch oven, heat the oil over medium heat. When it shimmers, add the sausage. Cook, stirring to break up, until no longer pink. Add the bell pepper, onion, and garlic. Continue cooking for 6 to 8 minutes, stirring occasionally, until the sausage is browned and the vegetables have softened.

2. Add the tomatoes, stock, and salt. Bring to a boil and add the pasta. Reduce the heat to a simmer and cook until the pasta is done, about 10 to 12 minutes. Stir in the parsley and black pepper.

3. Divide the mozzarella between 4 large bowls and ladle the soup over the cheese. Top with a scoop of ricotta and sprinkle with the Parmesan.

HELPFUL HINT: If you want a zestier dish, use hot Italian sausage, and mix the ricotta with black pepper, Italian herbs, and a hint of garlic.

PER SERVING: Calories: 904; Total fat: 50g; Carbohydrates: 66g; Fiber: 8.5g; Protein: 44g; Sodium: 1,697mg

SAUSAGE and CHICKEN JAMBALAYA

ACTIVE TIME: 15 minutes
TOTAL TIME: 45 minutes

Sort of an enriched rice pilaf, jambalaya is one of Louisiana's best-known dishes. This version combines spicy andouille sausage and chicken with the rice for a hearty, savory dinner. **SERVES 4**

2 tablespoons olive oil

1 pound boneless skinless chicken thighs, cut into 1-inch chunks

8 ounces andouille sausage, cut into ½-inch slices

1 small onion

½ medium green bell pepper, seeded and chopped

1 small celery stalk, chopped

2 large garlic cloves, minced

1½ teaspoons Cajun or Creole seasoning

1½ cups long-grain white rice

2½ cups low-sodium chicken stock

1 (14.5-ounce) can diced tomatoes

2 tablespoons chopped fresh parsley or other fresh herbs

4 lemon wedges

1. In a Dutch oven, heat the oil over medium-high heat. When it shimmers, add the chicken and sausage. Cook, stirring occasionally, for 5 to 7 minutes or until browned. Remove sausage and chicken and set aside.

2. Add the onion, pepper, celery, garlic, and seasoning to the pot. Cook, stirring, for 5 minutes or until the vegetables are tender.

3. Stir in the rice to coat with oil. Add the stock, tomatoes and their juices, chicken, and sausage. Bring to a boil. Stir, then cover the pot and reduce the heat to low. Cook for 20 minutes, or until rice is tender.

4. Fluff gently and garnish with parsley and lemon.

HELPFUL HINT: Since the sausage, seasoning mix, tomatoes, and stock can have varying amounts of sodium, it's best not to add any salt until after cooking, when you can taste first, then adjust.

PER SERVING: Calories: 608; Total fat: 19g; Carbohydrates: 65g; Fiber: 2.5g; Protein: 43g; Sodium: 846mg

CREAMY CHICKEN and NOODLES

NUT-FREE

ACTIVE TIME: 20 minutes

TOTAL TIME: 40 minutes

Dredging and frying the chicken might seem time-consuming, but it adds tons of flavor and texture to this comfort-food classic. SERVES 4

½ cup flour

½ teaspoon kosher salt

⅛ teaspoon
  ground cayenne

⅛ teaspoon black pepper

1¼ pounds boneless
  skinless chicken thighs

¼ cup vegetable oil

4 cups low-sodium
  chicken stock

3 large carrots, cut into
  ½-inch thick slices

2 large celery stalks, cut
  into ½-inch thick slices

1 bay leaf

1 cup frozen pearl
  onions, thawed

6 ounces egg noodles

⅔ cup frozen peas, thawed

¼ cup heavy cream

1. In a shallow dish, mix together the flour, salt, cayenne, and black pepper. Dredge the chicken in the flour mixture, coating both sides. Reserve the excess flour.

2. In a Dutch oven, heat the oil over medium-high heat. When shimmering, add the chicken in a single layer, working in batches, if needed. Cook without moving for 4 to 5 minutes, or until golden brown. Flip and cook for 3 to 4 minutes, or until browned. Transfer the chicken to a cutting board and let cool for a few minutes, then cut into bite-size pieces.

3. Add 1 tablespoon of the reserved flour mixture to the pot and stir, cooking, for 1 to 2 minutes, or until the flour is browned slightly. Add the stock and bring to a simmer for 4 to 5 minutes to thicken.

4. Add the carrots, celery, and bay leaf and cook for 6 to 8 minutes, until softened.

5. Bring the mixture to a boil and add the pearl onions and noodles. Cook for 10 to 12 minutes, or until the noodles are done, then add the chicken, peas, and cream. Cook for 2 to 3 minutes to warm the chicken and soften the peas. Remove the bay leaf and serve.

EASY SUB: To make the dish dairy-free, just leave out the cream.

PER SERVING: Calories: 509; Total fat: 25g; Carbohydrates: 30g; Fiber: 4g; Protein: 40g; Sodium: 372mg

GARLIC POT ROAST with MUSHROOMS

ACTIVE TIME: 15 minutes
TOTAL TIME: 2 hours

This dish has all the delicious comfort of pot roast, but with a twist. Whole cloves of garlic flavor the meat and sauce, while mushrooms and potatoes round out the meal. **SERVES 4**

1 (2½-pound) beef
　shoulder roast
1 teaspoon kosher salt
½ teaspoon black pepper
1 tablespoon vegetable oil
½ cup dry white wine
1 cup low-sodium
　beef broth
1 teaspoon Worcestershire
　sauce
1 medium onion, quartered
1 head garlic, cloves
　separated and peeled
2 sprigs fresh thyme or
　1 teaspoon dried thyme
1 pound small red or
　Yukon Gold potatoes,
　1 to 2 inches in diameter
1½ cups quartered
　cremini mushrooms

1. Preheat the oven to 325°F.

2. Sprinkle the roast on all sides with the salt and pepper.

3. In a Dutch oven, heat the oil over medium heat until shimmering. Brown the roast on all sides, about 8 minutes total. Transfer to a plate. Add the wine and bring to a simmer, scraping up the browned bits. Stir in the broth and Worcestershire sauce. Add the onion, garlic, and thyme. Place the roast in the liquid.

4. Place in the oven with the lid ajar. Cook for 1 hour to 90 minutes, or until the roast is barely tender. Add the potatoes and mushrooms.

5. Return to the oven uncovered. Cook for another 30 to 40 minutes, or until the vegetables are tender and the beef pulls apart easily with a fork.

HELPFUL HINT: Beef shoulder (chuck) comprises several different muscles, which is why it's difficult to predict exactly how long a particular cut will take to cook. It's best to check it several times during cooking.

PER SERVING: Calories: 545; Total fat: 19g; Carbohydrates: 26g; Fiber: 2.5g; Protein: 64g; Sodium: 547mg

CHICKEN PAPRIKASH with POTATOES

ACTIVE TIME: 20 minutes
TOTAL TIME: 1 hour

There are lots of versions of this Hungarian dish. Mine adds potatoes to the peppers and chicken to make a one-pot meal that would, I hope, make any Hungarian grandmother proud. **SERVES 4**

2 teaspoons kosher salt

2 pounds chicken wings, thighs, and drumsticks

3 tablespoons olive oil, divided

1 onion, chopped

1 large red bell pepper, seeded and sliced

3 tablespoons sweet paprika

1½ cups low-sodium chicken stock

12 ounces red potatoes, cut into ¼-inch-thick slices

½ cup fresh parsley leaves

PER SERVING: Calories: 529; Total fat: 37g; Carbohydrates: 19g; Fiber: 2.5g; Protein: 28g; Sodium: 736mg

1. Preheat the oven to 350°F.

2. Salt the chicken on all sides.

3. In a Dutch oven, heat 2 tablespoons of the oil over medium-high heat until shimmering. Brown the chicken, skin-side down, for 4 to 6 minutes. Flip and brown for 2 to 3 minutes. If necessary, work in batches with half the oil for each batch. Transfer the chicken to a plate or cutting board.

4. In the Dutch oven, heat the remaining 1 tablespoon of oil over medium-high heat. Cook the onion for 2 to 3 minutes, stirring. Add the bell pepper and cook for 2 to 3 minutes. Stir in the paprika and cook for 1 minute. Add the stock and bring to a simmer. Add the potatoes and parsley. Place the chicken pieces on top.

5. Bake, covered, for 20 minutes. Turn the oven up to 400°F.

6. Transfer the chicken to a plate or cutting board. Blot off any fat on the top of the sauce, and gently stir the potatoes and peppers. Return the chicken to the pot.

7. Bake, uncovered, for 20 minutes, until the chicken skin is crisp.

HELPFUL HINT: This dish is traditionally made with Hungarian paprika, but any type is fine, so long as it's sweet—that is, not hot paprika, which will set your taste buds on fire.

MOROCCAN CHICKEN and SWEET POTATOES

DAIRY-FREE | GLUTEN-FREE | NUT-FREE

ACTIVE TIME: 15 minutes
TOTAL TIME: 55 minutes

Cumin, coriander, and oranges flavor this crisp chicken and sweet potato dish. Removing the orange segments from the membrane takes a little practice, but it results in an elegant dish. SERVES 4

4 large bone-in, skin-on
   chicken thighs
   (6 to 7 ounces each)
1¼ teaspoons kosher
   salt, divided
1 tablespoon olive oil
1 small onion, sliced
2 garlic cloves, minced
1 tablespoon
   ground cumin
2 teaspoons
   ground coriander
½ cup dry white wine
1 cup low-sodium
   chicken stock
1 tablespoon orange
   juice concentrate
1 pound sweet potatoes,
   peeled and cut into
   ¼-inch-thick slices
1 large orange,
   membrane removed
½ cup coarsely chopped
   Kalamata olives

PER SERVING: Calories: 363;
Total fat: 13g; Carbohydrates:
32g; Fiber: 4.5g; Protein: 24g;
Sodium: 828mg

1. Preheat the oven to 300°F. Sprinkle the chicken with 1 teaspoon of the salt.

2. In a Dutch oven, heat the oil over medium heat. Cook the chicken, skin-side down, for 5 to 6 minutes. Flip and cook for 4 to 5 minutes, until browned. Set aside.

3. Cook the onion in the pot for 3 to 4 minutes, until slightly browned. Add the garlic, cumin, and coriander and cook for 1 minute. Add the wine and stir to dissolve the browned bits on the bottom of the pot. Reduce by half.

4. Add the stock, orange juice concentrate, and remaining ¼ teaspoon of salt. Bring to a simmer. Add the sweet potatoes in an even layer and place the chicken on top, skin-side up. Cover and bake for 20 minutes.

5. Meanwhile, over a bowl, cut the orange segments from the membranes.

6. Remove the pot from the oven and raise the temperature to 400°F. Remove the chicken and set aside. Blot off any fat and gently stir the sweet potatoes. Add the orange segments and juices from the bowl and the olives. Return the chicken to the pot, skin-side up.

7. Bake for 15 or 20 minutes, uncovered, until the chicken skin is crisp.

EASY SUB: You can use Yukon Gold or red potatoes, sliced or quartered, in place of the sweet potatoes.

CREOLE WHITE BEANS and HAM

ACTIVE TIME: 15 minutes
TOTAL TIME: 45 minutes

Creole mustard and Cajun seasoning are the keys to this New Orleans–influenced stew. The finished dish is spicy with a little kick. If you like it less hot, omit the pepper sauce, or pass it at the table. SERVES 4

1 tablespoon olive oil

1 small onion, chopped

3 garlic cloves, minced

4 cups low-sodium chicken broth

2 (15-ounce) cans navy or other white beans, drained and rinsed

1 (14.5-ounce) can diced tomatoes

1½ cups diced ham

2 carrots, chopped

3 tablespoons Creole mustard or other whole-grain mustard

2 teaspoons Worcestershire sauce

1 teaspoon Creole or Cajun seasoning

½ teaspoon hot sauce

3 cups arugula, loosely packed

1. In a Dutch oven, heat the oil over medium heat. When it shimmers, add the onion and cook, stirring, for 3 to 4 minutes, or until softened. Add the garlic and cook for a minute, until fragrant.

2. Add the broth, beans, tomatoes and their juices, ham, carrots, mustard, Worcestershire sauce, seasoning, and hot sauce. Bring to a simmer.

3. Turn the heat to low and cover the pot. Simmer, stirring occasionally, for 30 minutes, or until the carrots are tender. Add the arugula and stir to wilt the greens.

HELPFUL HINT: If you can find a small chunk of cooked ham in the meat section, that's your best choice for this dish. If not, ask the deli clerk to cut ham in slices about ½-inch thick and use that.

PER SERVING: Calories: 443; Total fat: 6.5g; Carbohydrates: 60g; Fiber: 14g; Protein: 34g; Sodium: 1,802mg

SNAPPER VERACRUZ

DAIRY-FREE | **GLUTEN-FREE** | **NUT-FREE**

ACTIVE TIME: 15 minutes
TOTAL TIME: 45 minutes

Traditionally made with a whole snapper, Snapper Veracruz is just as delicious with fillets. The addition of beans to the savory sauce of tomatoes, olives, and capers turns a flavorful entrée into a complete meal. SERVES 4

4 (6-ounce) snapper fillets

1 teaspoon kosher
   salt, divided

½ teaspoon black pepper

3 tablespoons olive oil

1 small onion, sliced

2 large garlic
   cloves, minced

1 jalapeño, seeded
   and minced

2 (15-ounce) cans
   pinto beans, drained
   and rinsed

1 (14.5-ounce) can diced
   tomatoes, drained

¼ cup sliced green olives

½ teaspoon dried oregano

3 tablespoons capers

2 tablespoons
   chopped parsley

1. Sprinkle the fish on both sides with ¾ teaspoon of the salt and the pepper.

2. In a Dutch oven, heat the oil over medium heat. When it shimmers, add the onion and cook for 3 to 4 minutes, or until beginning to brown. Add the garlic and jalapeño and cook for 1 to 2 minutes, or until the garlic is fragrant.

3. Add the beans, tomatoes, olives, oregano, and the remaining ¼ teaspoon of salt and stir to combine. Bring to a simmer and cook, partially covered, for 15 to 20 minutes, or until slightly thickened.

4. Place the fish in the pot, and scoop some of the sauce over the fillets. Return to a simmer and cover the pot. Cook for 15 minutes, or until the fish flakes with a fork. Garnish with the capers and parsley and serve.

EASY SUB: Any mild whitefish can be used in place of the snapper. Grouper, cod, and tilapia all work well.

PER SERVING: Calories: 464; Total fat: 15g; Carbohydrates: 36g; Fiber: 9.5g; Protein: 45g; Sodium: 1,216mg

MUSTARD-SPIKED BEEF STEW

DAIRY-FREE | **NUT-FREE**

ACTIVE TIME: 15 minutes

TOTAL TIME: 1 hour 20 minutes

This stew gets its deep flavor from the technique of browning large pieces of meat, then cutting them—less liquid escapes, so you get a more flavorful base to build a sauce. If you buy stew meat, just brown it and proceed with the recipe.

SERVES 4

1 (1½-pound) boneless beef shoulder roast, cut into 2 (1½-inch-thick) slices

½ teaspoon kosher salt

2 tablespoons vegetable oil

¾ cup dry red wine

1½ cups low-sodium beef stock

1 tablespoon all-purpose flour

1 small onion, peeled and quartered

2 tablespoons whole-grain mustard

2 medium garlic cloves

1 bay leaf

10 ounces Yukon Gold potatoes, cut into 2-inch cubes

3 carrots, cut into 1-inch pieces

¼ teaspoon black pepper

1. Sprinkle the beef with the salt.

2. In a Dutch oven, heat the oil over medium. Brown the beef for 3 minutes. Flip and brown for 3 more minutes. Transfer to a plate and set aside.

3. Pour the wine in the pot and stir, scraping up any browned bits. Bring to a boil and cook for 1 to 2 minutes, or until reduced by about a third.

4. Meanwhile, cut the beef into 1-inch cubes.

5. In a small bowl, whisk together the stock and flour. Add to the pot, along with the onion, mustard, garlic, and bay leaf. Add the beef and bring to a simmer. Cover and turn the heat to low.

6. Cook for about 40 minutes, until the beef is tender but not falling apart. Remove the onion, bay leaf, and garlic. Add the potatoes, carrots, and black pepper, and cook for about 30 more minutes, until the vegetables are tender.

HELPFUL HINT: If necessary, cook the beef in two batches. You'll get better browning if you don't crowd the pot.

PER SERVING: Calories: 422; Total fat: 16g; Carbohydrates: 21g; Fiber: 3g; Protein: 39g; Sodium: 519mg

HONEY-MUSTARD CHICKEN with POTATOES and SPROUTS

ACTIVE TIME: 15 minutes
TOTAL TIME: 1 hour 15 minutes

Roasting a whole chicken over potatoes and Brussels sprouts imbues the vegetables with wonderful flavor, while also lifting the chicken up a bit in the pot so that it can brown more readily. **SERVES 4**

1 (4-pound) whole
   roasting chicken
3 teaspoons kosher
   salt, divided
1 pound Brussels
   sprouts, trimmed
1 pound small
   red potatoes
1 tablespoon vegetable oil
2 tablespoons
   Dijon mustard
1 tablespoon honey

1. Preheat the oven to 400°F.

2. Pat the chicken dry and salt inside and out with 2 teaspoons of the salt.

3. In a Dutch oven, combine the Brussels sprouts and potatoes and drizzle with the oil. Sprinkle with the remaining 1 teaspoon of salt and toss.

4. Place the chicken on the vegetables, breast-side up.

5. Roast, uncovered, for 30 minutes. Remove the pot from the oven, transfer the chicken to a cutting board, and toss the vegetables.

6. In a small bowl, mix together the mustard and honey and brush over the chicken breasts, legs, and thighs.

7. Place the chicken back in the pot, return the pot to the oven, and roast for another 20 to 40 minutes, or until the thigh meat registers 165°F on a meat thermometer and the juices run clear.

EASY SUB: Skip the honey mustard and use your favorite barbecue sauce to glaze the chicken.

PER SERVING: Calories: 697; Total fat: 33g; Carbohydrates: 32g; Fiber: 6g; Protein: 65g; Sodium: 1,246mg

SOUTHWESTERN BLACK BEAN
and CORN STEW

GLUTEN-FREE   NUT-FREE   VEGETARIAN

ACTIVE TIME: 15 minutes
TOTAL TIME: 40 minutes

Colorful vegetables and hearty beans make this stew as pretty as it is delicious. Reminiscent of chili, it'll warm you up on cool nights. SERVES 4

2 tablespoons
  vegetable oil

1 onion, chopped

1 red bell pepper,
  seeded and cut into
  ½-inch chunks

1 green bell pepper,
  seeded and cut into
  ½-inch chunks

1 jalapeño, minced

2 garlic cloves, minced

3 tablespoons chili powder

1 teaspoon ground cumin

1 teaspoon dried oregano

2 (15-ounce) cans
  black beans, drained
  and rinsed

2 cups frozen corn

2 cups vegetable stock

1 (14.5-ounce) can
  diced tomatoes

½ teaspoon kosher salt

¼ cup chopped
  fresh cilantro

1 avocado, pitted, peeled,
  and chopped

1 cup shredded Monterey
  Jack cheese

1. In a Dutch oven, heat the oil over medium heat. When it shimmers, add the onion, bell peppers, jalapeño, and garlic. Cook for 5 to 6 minutes, stirring, until the vegetables start to soften. Stir in the chili powder, cumin, and oregano and cook for a minute, or until fragrant.

2. Add the beans, corn, stock, tomatoes and their juices, and salt.

3. Bring to a simmer and cook, partially covered, for 20 to 25 minutes. Stir in the cilantro and avocado and serve immediately, garnished with the cheese.

HELPFUL HINT: Beans, vegetable stock, and canned tomatoes can all vary in sodium, so start with just ½ teaspoon of kosher salt and then add more if necessary.

PER SERVING: Calories: 535; Total fat: 23g; Carbohydrates: 64g; Fiber: 21g; Protein: 24g; Sodium: 1,532mg

GREEK-STYLE ROASTED VEGETABLES
with BULGUR WHEAT

ACTIVE TIME: 15 minutes
TOTAL TIME: 50 minutes

Mixed roasted vegetables tossed in a vinaigrette and accented with feta and olives is a favorite of mine. Adding bulgur wheat turns the dish into a delicious light dinner. SERVES 4

¾ cup bulgur wheat

1 teaspoon kosher
    salt, divided

1 red or yellow bell pepper,
    seeded and cut into
    1-inch chunks

1 small onion, cut into
    ¼-inch wedges

4 tablespoons olive oil,
    divided

2 medium zucchini or
    summer squash, cut into
    ¼-inch-thick
    half-moons

1 cup halved
    cherry tomatoes

1 garlic clove, minced
    or pressed

2 tablespoons lemon juice

½ teaspoon dried oregano

½ teaspoon black pepper

½ cup crumbled
    feta cheese

¼ cup toasted pine nuts

3 tablespoons coarsely
    chopped Kalamata olives

1. Preheat the oven to 375°F.

2. In a Dutch oven, cover the bulgur with about ½ inch of water. Stir in ¼ teaspoon of the salt. Bring to a boil, then turn off the heat and cover the pot. Let sit for 5 minutes, then drain in a colander or sieve.

3. In the Dutch oven, combine the bell pepper and onion. Drizzle with 1 tablespoon of oil and sprinkle with ½ teaspoon of the salt.

4. Place the pot in the oven and roast for 15 to 20 minutes, or until the vegetables begin to brown.

5. Remove the pot and add the zucchini, tomatoes, and garlic. Drizzle with another tablespoon of oil and sprinkle with the remaining ¼ teaspoon of salt.

6. Return to the oven and roast for 15 to 20 minutes, until the zucchini is tender and the tomatoes have begun to collapse.

7. Remove from the oven and add the bulgur. Cool for several minutes.

8. Add the remaining 2 tablespoons of olive oil, lemon juice, oregano, and black pepper. Toss gently. Garnish with the feta, pine nuts, and olives.

EASY SUB: For a gluten-free version, substitute quinoa or rice for the bulgur.

PER SERVING: Calories: 371; Total fat: 26g; Carbohydrates: 30g; Fiber: 6g; Protein: 9g; Sodium: 433mg

BEER-BRAISED KIELBASA and VEGETABLES

ACTIVE TIME: 15 minutes
TOTAL TIME: 40 minutes

Maybe it's my German heritage, but nothing says comfort food to me like smoked sausage braised with cabbage and potatoes. Beer, mustard, and caraway seeds flavor the braising liquid, resulting in a savory sauce that's the perfect complement for the dish. SERVES 4

1 tablespoon vegetable oil

½ medium onion, cut through the stem and root

1 (13-ounce) kielbasa or other smoked sausage, cut into 1½-inch lengths

¾ cup beer

1¼ cups low-sodium chicken stock

2 tablespoons whole-grain mustard

1 tablespoon flour

2 garlic cloves, minced or pressed

1 teaspoon kosher salt

½ teaspoon caraway seeds

¼ teaspoon black pepper

½ small cabbage (about 1 pound)

1 pound small red potatoes, quartered

3 large carrots, cut into ½-inch pieces

1. In a Dutch oven, heat the oil over medium heat until shimmering. While it heats, cut the onion into 8 wedges. Add the sausage and onion and cook, stirring occasionally, until the sausage is browned, about 3 minutes.

2. Add the beer and cook for 4 to 5 minutes, until it's reduced by half.

3. While it reduces, in a small bowl, whisk together the stock, mustard, flour, garlic, salt, caraway, and black pepper. Add to the pot and bring to a simmer.

4. While it heats, quarter the cabbage through the core. Add the potatoes and carrots to the pot and stir. Lay the cabbage wedges on top to steam.

5. Cover and simmer for 25 to 30 minutes, or until the vegetables are tender.

SIMPLE SUB: For a gluten-free version, use dry white wine instead of beer, and substitute 2 teaspoons cornstarch for the flour.

PER SERVING: Calories: 408; Total fat: 20g; Carbohydrates: 35g; Fiber: 6.5g; Protein: 21g; Sodium: 1,287mg

CHILI-CHEESE-TATER TOT CASSEROLE

GLUTEN-FREE NUT-FREE

ACTIVE TIME: 20 minutes

TOTAL TIME: 40 minutes

In this recipe, my ode to chili cheese fries, the tater tots are lightly fried and then become deep golden brown and crisp as they bake on top of the chili. SERVES 4

Vegetable oil, for frying

3 cups frozen tater tots

1 pound ground
beef (80/20)

1 medium onion, chopped

1 jalapeño pepper,
chopped

1 teaspoon kosher salt

6 tablespoons ancho
chili powder

1 tablespoon
ground cumin

2 teaspoons minced garlic

½ teaspoon dried oregano

1 (15-ounce) can pinto
beans, drained
and rinsed

1 (14.5-ounce) can
diced tomatoes

1 cup shredded Monterey
Jack cheese

1 cup shredded
cheddar cheese

1. Preheat the oven to 375°F.

2. In a Dutch oven, heat an inch of oil over medium heat to 365°F. Fry the tater tots in a single layer until lightly browned. Using a slotted spoon, transfer to paper towels. Discard the oil.

3. In the Dutch oven, cook the beef over medium heat for 3 to 4 minutes, stirring. Add the onion and jalapeño. Sprinkle with the salt and cook for another 5 to 6 minutes, until the beef is browned. If there is more than a tablespoon of fat in the pot, drain or blot it off.

4. Add the chili powder, cumin, garlic, and oregano, and cook for 1 to 2 minutes. Stir in the beans and tomatoes and their juices. Remove from the heat.

5. Sprinkle the cheeses over the chili and top with the tater tots in a single layer.

6. Bake for 20 to 22 minutes, or until golden brown.

7. Remove from the oven. If oil from the cheese is pooled along the sides, blot it off before serving.

EASY SUB: If you have a favorite chili recipe, feel free to substitute it for mine. Just make sure it's not too soupy, or the final dish will be messy.

PER SERVING: Calories: 760; Total fat: 44g; Carbohydrates: 50g; Fiber: 7g; Protein: 42g; Sodium: 1,528mg

LAMB SHANKS WITH WHITE BEANS (PAGE 73)

CHAPTER FIVE

Original Slow Cookers

Back in frontier days, a Dutch oven was often hung over a fire or nestled into coals to slow-cook stews, soups, and braised meats. Today, you can still use your Dutch oven for slow cooking—just not over a wood fire, please! Either in the oven or on the stove, a Dutch oven heats evenly and holds a low, steady temperature, which is perfect for long-simmering dishes.

SPICY CHICKPEA STEW

ACTIVE TIME: 15 minutes

TOTAL TIME: 2 hours 15 minutes

Chickpeas, or garbanzo beans, are a favorite in numerous cuisines, notably around the Mediterranean. You might be most familiar with them pureed into hummus, but they're a great base for stew, especially when assertively spiced, as in this recipe. SERVES 4

1 pound dried chickpeas, sorted and rinsed

2 teaspoons kosher salt, divided

2 tablespoons olive oil

1 small onion, chopped

4 garlic cloves, minced

2 jalapeños, chopped

1 tablespoon hot curry powder

4 cups low-sodium vegetable stock

1 (14.5-ounce) can diced tomatoes

4 cups packed baby spinach

1. In a Dutch oven, cover the chickpeas with 2 inches of water. Add 1 teaspoon of the salt and place over high heat. Bring to a boil and cook for 1 minute, then remove from heat, cover the pot, and let rest for 1 hour. Drain the chickpeas in a colander and wipe out the pot.

2. Preheat the oven to 325°F.

3. In the Dutch oven, heat the oil over medium-high heat. When the oil shimmers, add the onion and the remaining teaspoon of salt. Cook, stirring, for 5 to 6 minutes, or until browned. Add the garlic, jalapeños, and curry powder and cook for another minute, or until fragrant.

4. Add the stock and tomatoes and their juices and stir to combine. Add the chickpeas.

5. Place the pot in the oven, lid slightly ajar. Cook for about an hour, or until the chickpeas are tender. Stir in the spinach to wilt, and serve.

HELPFUL HINT: If you have the time, you can soak the chickpeas overnight in 1 quart water mixed with 1 tablespoon kosher salt, skipping step 1. Drain and rinse, then continue with step 2.

PER SERVING: Calories: 514; Total fat: 13g; Carbohydrates: 78g; Fiber: 21g; Protein: 24g; Sodium: 874mg

LAMB SHANKS with WHITE BEANS

ACTIVE TIME: 20 minutes

TOTAL TIME: 3 hours

A combination of lamb, beans, and tomatoes was first introduced to me by food writer and journalist Russ Parsons. This recipe does take some initial work, but it can then cook mostly unattended. **SERVES 4**

4 pounds lamb shanks
  (4 to 6 shanks)
3 teaspoons kosher
  salt, divided
2 tablespoons olive oil
½ cup dry white wine
2 cups low-sodium
  chicken stock
1⅔ cups dry cannellini or
  white northern beans
1 (14.5-ounce) can
  diced tomatoes
1 medium onion, quartered
2 garlic cloves, peeled
1 bay leaf
½ teaspoon black pepper
1 cup pitted green olives
¼ cup chopped parsley

1. Preheat the oven to 325°F.

2. Sprinkle the lamb with 2 teaspoons of the salt.

3. In a Dutch oven, heat the oil over medium-high heat. When the oil shimmers, add the lamb and brown for 3 to 4 minutes, working in batches if necessary. Transfer the lamb to a cutting board when browned.

4. Add the wine to the pot and bring to a simmer, scraping up the browned bits from the pot. Let the wine reduce by about half.

5. Add the lamb shanks, stock, beans, tomatoes and their juices, onion, garlic, bay leaf, remaining 1 teaspoon of salt, and black pepper. Bring to a simmer.

6. Cover the pot and place in the oven. Cook for an hour, then set the lid ajar and continue cooking for another 30 minutes to 1 hour. Check the beans and lamb; they should be tender. Continue cooking if necessary.

7. Before serving, remove the bay leaf and any chunks of onion or garlic, if visible. To serve, garnish with the olives and parsley.

EASY SUB: If you can't find lamb shanks, lamb shoulder chops also work in this recipe.

PER SERVING: Calories: 934; Total fat: 42g; Carbohydrates: 54g; Fiber: 28g; Protein: 80g; Sodium: 1,706mg

COQ AU VIN

ACTIVE TIME: 20 minutes

TOTAL TIME: 2 hours

This classic French dish was traditionally made with tough old rooster, which required a long soak in wine to become tender. The process is streamlined in this modern version. SERVES 4

4 pounds chicken
　drumsticks and thighs
2 teaspoons kosher
　salt, divided
4 slices bacon, diced
2 cups quartered
　white mushrooms
1 cup frozen pearl
　onions, thawed
1 small onion, sliced
1 tablespoon tomato paste
2 cups dry red wine
1 cup low-sodium
　chicken stock
1 teaspoon brown sugar
¼ teaspoon black pepper
2 carrots, cut into
　½-inch coins

1. Preheat the oven to 300°F.

2. Cut through the tendon on each chicken leg to release the meat, if preferred. Sprinkle chicken with 1 teaspoon of the salt.

3. In a Dutch oven, cook the bacon over medium-low heat for 5 to 6 minutes, stirring occasionally, until crisp. Using a slotted spoon, transfer the bacon to a paper-towel-lined plate. Cook the mushrooms and pearl onions for 5 to 6 minutes, stirring occasionally, until lightly browned. Transfer to the plate with the bacon.

4. Add the chicken, skin-side down, and sear for 4 to 6 minutes, working in batches if necessary. Remove from the pot and set aside.

5. Add the onion and tomato paste, cooking for 4 to 5 minutes, until softened. Stir in the wine, stock, sugar, black pepper, and bacon. Bring to a simmer. Return the chicken to the pot, skin-side up.

6. Place the pot in the oven with the lid ajar. Cook for 1 hour, then add the carrots. Cook for another 30 minutes, or until the chicken is tender.

CONTINUED

7. Remove from the oven, take the chicken out of the pot, and set aside.

8. Using a fat separator or spoon, remove as much grease as possible. Bring to a simmer for 8 to 12 minutes, until reduced. Stir in the mushrooms and pearl onions to heat through. Add the chicken to reheat.

HELPFUL HINT: If you like crisp skin on your chicken, you can run the pieces under the broiler while the sauce reduces.

PER SERVING: Calories: 886; Total fat: 52g; Carbohydrates: 16g; Fiber: 2g; Protein: 65g; Sodium: 1,029mg

SALMON with SLOW-ROASTED VEGETABLES

ACTIVE TIME: 20 minutes

TOTAL TIME: 1 hour 45 minutes

Slow-roasting onions in the oven turns them meltingly soft, with complex sweet and savory flavors. Add peppers and tomatoes, and you have a fabulous accompaniment for roasted salmon fillets. The vegetables both flavor the salmon and protect it from overcooking, resulting in an easy, almost foolproof dinner.

SERVES 4

2 tablespoons olive oil

2 tablespoons
   unsalted butter

1 pound onions, sliced

2 teaspoons kosher
   salt, divided

2 thyme sprigs (or
   1 teaspoon dried thyme)

1 pint cherry
   tomatoes, halved

1 yellow bell pepper,
   seeded and sliced

4 (6-ounce) salmon fillets

¼ teaspoon black pepper

1. Preheat the oven to 325°F.

2. In a Dutch oven, heat the oil and butter over medium heat until foaming. Add the onions, sprinkle with 1 teaspoon of the salt, and cook, stirring, just until the onions are hot and begin to exude some liquid. Add the thyme.

3. Cover the pot and place it in the oven. Cook for 1 hour. Remove the pot and turn the oven up to 375°F.

4. Add the tomatoes and bell pepper. Stir. Return to the oven and cook, uncovered, for 30 minutes.

5. Sprinkle the salmon with the remaining 1 teaspoon of salt and the black pepper. Remove the pot from the oven, place the salmon in the pot, and spoon the vegetables over.

6. Return the pot to the oven and bake for 15 minutes, or until the salmon flakes apart with a fork.

SERVE IT WITH: Herbed Rice Pilaf (page 103) and Silky Garlic Mashed Potatoes (page 109) are both excellent complements to the fish.

PER SERVING: Calories: 423; Total fat: 24g; Carbohydrates: 16g; Fiber: 3g; Protein: 36g; Sodium: 645mg

CHUNKY SPLIT PEA SOUP

DAIRY-FREE | **GLUTEN-FREE** | **NUT-FREE**

ACTIVE TIME: 20 minutes
TOTAL TIME: 1 hour 40 minutes

Chunks of ham and vegetables works well in this soup to offset the silky texture of the peas. To keep the vegetables from turning to mush, add them partway through the cooking process. SERVES 4

1 tablespoon vegetable oil

1 small onion, chopped

2 garlic cloves, minced
   or pressed

8 cups water

1 pound dried split peas,
   rinsed and sorted

1 large (about 1 pound)
   smoked ham hock

2 bay leaves

1 teaspoon kosher salt

½ teaspoon dried thyme

2 medium carrots,
   thinly sliced

2 celery stalks,
   thinly sliced

2 tablespoons chopped
   fresh parsley

1 to 2 dashes
   Tabasco sauce

¼ teaspoon black pepper

1. Preheat the oven to 325°F.

2. In a Dutch oven, heat the oil over medium heat. When it shimmers, add the onion and garlic and cook for about 4 minutes, stirring, until softened. Add the water, peas, ham hock, bay leaves, salt, and thyme. Bring to a simmer, then cover the pot and transfer to the oven.

3. Cook for 1 hour. Remove the pot and add the carrots and celery. Return to the oven and cook, covered, for 30 to 40 minutes, or until the ham is very soft and the peas are dissolving.

4. Remove the ham hock and let sit until cool enough to handle. Remove the meat in chunks and return to the soup. Remove the bay leaves and stir in the parsley, Tabasco, and black pepper. Reheat if necessary.

EASY SUB: If you can't find a ham hock, you can use smoked turkey wings instead.

PER SERVING: Calories: 655; Total fat: 16g; Carbohydrates: 74g; Fiber: 29g; Protein: 53g; Sodium: 1,262mg

JAMAICAN RICE and PEAS

DAIRY-FREE **GLUTEN-FREE** **NUT-FREE** **VEGETARIAN**

ACTIVE TIME:
15 minutes

TOTAL TIME: 2 hours 30 minutes

The peas in Jamaican rice and peas are not peas at all, at least not what I think of as peas. Instead, the rice is paired with savory red beans, all cooked together with traditional Jamaican spices—ginger, garlic, thyme, and lots of allspice.

SERVES 4

1 cup dried
   red beans, rinsed

1 (13.5-ounce) can full-fat
   coconut milk

1 scallion, both white and
   green parts, cut into
   3 pieces

2 garlic cloves, peeled

2 thyme sprigs or
   1 teaspoon dried thyme

1 teaspoon ground allspice

2 teaspoons kosher
   salt, divided

½ teaspoon ground ginger

5 cups water, divided

1½ cups long-grain
   white rice

1. Preheat the oven to 325°F.

2. In a Dutch oven, combine the beans, coconut milk, scallion, garlic, thyme, allspice, 1 teaspoon of the salt, and ginger. Pour in 3 cups of water and stir to combine. Bring to a boil over medium heat, then reduce to a simmer. Cover the pot and place in the oven. Cook for 90 minutes, then check the beans. They should be tender; if necessary, continue cooking for another 30 minutes.

3. Remove the pot from the oven and raise the temperature to 350°F. Remove the garlic, scallion, and thyme. Stir in the rice with the remaining 2 cups of water and the remaining 1 teaspoon of salt. Cover and return to the oven.

4. Cook for 25 to 30 minutes, or until the rice is tender and most of the liquid is absorbed. Fluff with a fork before serving.

EASY SUB: This dish is usually made with red kidney beans, but not everyone cares for them, so feel free to substitute small red beans.

PER SERVING: Calories: 605; Total fat: 21g; Carbohydrates: 87g; Fiber: 9g; Protein: 17g; Sodium: 582mg

SHRIMP and SAUSAGE GUMBO

ACTIVE TIME: 20 minutes

TOTAL TIME: 2 hours

The New Orleans classic can include a wide variety of meat, poultry, or seafood. This version combines spicy andouille sausage with plump shrimp to serve over rice. SERVES 4

⅓ cup plus 1 tablespoon vegetable oil, divided

8 ounces andouille sausage, diced

⅓ cup all-purpose flour

1 small onion, chopped

1 small green bell pepper, seeded and chopped

1 celery stalk, chopped

2 garlic cloves, minced

1 tablespoon tomato paste

4 cups low-sodium chicken stock

1 tablespoon Worcestershire sauce

1 tablespoon Cajun seasoning

2 cups chopped fresh or frozen okra

1 pound (size 21/25) shrimp, peeled and deveined

PER SERVING: Calories: 651; Total fat: 46g; Carbohydrates: 18g; Fiber: 2.5g; Protein: 41g; Sodium: 744mg

1. In a Dutch oven, heat 1 tablespoon of the oil over medium heat. When shimmering, cook the sausage for 3 to 5 minutes, stirring occasionally, until browned, then remove. Scrape any browned bits off the bottom of the pot and wipe it out.

2. Heat the remaining ⅓ cup of oil in the pot over medium high heat. When shimmering, add the flour while whisking. Reduce the heat to medium and stir for 6 minutes, until the roux turns light brown, like peanut butter. Add the onion and stir for another 5 minutes, until dark brown. Turn off the heat.

3. Add the bell pepper, celery, garlic, and tomato paste. Stir, cooking in the residual heat, for about 3 minutes, then add the stock. Bring to a boil over medium heat, then reduce the heat to low.

4. Add the sausage, Worcestershire sauce, and seasoning. Simmer, partially covered, for 50 minutes to 1 hour.

5. Add the okra and simmer for 30 minutes.

6. Add the shrimp and cook for 2 to 3 minutes, until cooked through.

HELPFUL HINT: The method for making the roux quickly over high heat comes from Louisiana chef Paul Prudhomme. While it requires close attention, it saves a lot of time over slow-cooked methods.

PORK CHILI VERDE with RICE

DAIRY-FREE | **GLUTEN-FREE** | **NUT-FREE**

ACTIVE TIME: 20 minutes
TOTAL TIME: 2 hours

Making this dish with a good-quality tomatillo salsa reduces the time without sacrificing flavor. I cook the rice right in the sauce for a savory accompaniment to the tender, spicy pork. SERVES 4

2 pounds boneless pork
   shoulder, cut into
   3-inch strips

1½ teaspoons kosher
   salt, divided

1 tablespoon vegetable oil

1 cup tomatillo salsa

½ cup low-sodium
   chicken stock

1 poblano chile, seeded
   and chopped

1 cup long-grain white rice

¼ cup chopped
   fresh cilantro

1. Sprinkle the pork with 1 teaspoon of the salt.

2. In a Dutch oven, heat the oil over medium heat. Brown the pork for 3 to 4 minutes. Flip the pieces and add the salsa, stock, and poblano and stir.

3. Set the oven to 250°F. Transfer the Dutch oven to the oven with the lid ajar. Cook for 1 hour.

4. Increase the heat to 300°F and remove the lid. Cook for 30 to 50 minutes longer, until the pork is tender.

5. Remove the pot from the oven. Transfer the pork to a cutting board. Blot off the fat from the sauce. Pour the sauce into a measuring cup; you should have at least 2 cups. If less, add salsa to make 2 cups. Return the sauce to the pot and add the rice and remaining ½ teaspoon of salt.

6. Bring to a boil over medium. Reduce to low and cover. Cook for 20 minutes.

7. Meanwhile, pull the pork into bite-size chunks.

8. After 20 minutes, check the rice. It should be tender, with most of the liquid absorbed. Stir in the pork and the cilantro.

9. Let warm for 2 to 3 minutes before serving.

EASY SUB: If you can't find pork shoulder, country ribs are great, too. Just be sure not to get country ribs from the loin, as the meat will dry out. Shoulder country ribs will be dark in color, with plenty of fat.

PER SERVING: Calories: 664; Total fat: 32g; Carbohydrates: 42g; Fiber: 1g; Protein: 47g; Sodium: 1,123mg

PORK RIBS CACCIATORE

DAIRY-FREE | GLUTEN-FREE | NUT-FREE

ACTIVE TIME: 25 minutes

TOTAL TIME: 4 hours 25 minutes

While chicken cacciatore gets all the press, its lesser-known cousin, the pork rib version, is just as delicious. These are fabulous served over the Silky Garlic Mashed Potatoes (page 109) or Roasted Red Pepper Polenta (page 112). **SERVES 4**

1 rack pork back ribs, cut into 2-rib sections

2 teaspoons kosher salt, divided

2 tablespoons olive oil

1½ cups sliced cremini mushrooms

1 small onion, sliced

2 garlic cloves, minced

½ cup dry red wine

1 (14.5-ounce) can diced tomatoes

1 cup low-sodium chicken stock

1 teaspoon dried oregano

2 tablespoons chopped fresh parsley

2 tablespoons capers

1. Salt the ribs with 1 teaspoon of the salt.

2. In a Dutch oven, heat the oil over medium-high heat. When the oil shimmers, add the ribs and brown on one side for 4 to 5 minutes, working in batches if necessary. Transfer to a plate.

3. Add the mushrooms, onion, garlic, and remaining 1 teaspoon of salt to the pot. Cook, stirring, until the vegetables begin to brown, about 3 minutes. Add the wine, scraping the bottom to release the browned bits. Boil until reduced by about half. Add the tomatoes and their juices, stock, and oregano.

4. Set the oven to 200°F. Transfer the pot to the oven with the lid ajar. Cook for 1 hour, then increase the heat to 250°F. Cook for 1 hour and 30 minutes. Increase the temperature to 300°F and cook for 1 hour to 1 hour and 30 minutes, or until ribs are very tender.

5. Remove the ribs from the pot and remove as much fat as possible from the sauce using a fat separator or a spoon. Return the ribs to the pot. Stir in the parsley and capers.

HELPFUL HINT: If you prefer a thicker sauce, simmer it over medium heat, uncovered, after removing the fat.

PER SERVING: Calories: 533; Total fat: 36g; Carbohydrates: 10g; Fiber: 1.5g; Protein: 37g; Sodium: 1,067mg

GREEN POSOLE with CHICKEN

ACTIVE TIME: 20 minutes
TOTAL TIME: 2 hours 20 minutes
(plus soaking)

In Mexico, the word *posole* (or *pozole*) is used both for the dried corn, hominy, and the stew that's made from it. Look for a package of the dried grain that notes it's already been nixtamalized or "prepared." SERVES 4

8 ounces dried
   prepared hominy
2 onions, sliced, divided
2 pounds skinless
   chicken drumsticks
1½ teaspoons kosher
   salt, divided
1 pound tomatillos, diced
½ cup fresh cilantro leaves
2 cups low-sodium
   chicken stock, divided
2 large poblano
   chiles, diced
1 medium jalapeño,
   chopped
2 garlic cloves, minced
1 teaspoon dried oregano
¼ teaspoon ground cumin

1. In a bowl, soak the hominy in cold water for 8 hours. Drain. Place the hominy in a Dutch oven with half of the onions. Add water to cover the hominy by 2 inches. Bring to a boil and cook for 5 minutes. Reduce the heat to low. When simmering, cover and cook for 1 hour, or until just becoming tender.

2. Meanwhile, sprinkle the chicken with 1 teaspoon of the salt.

3. Add the tomatillos, remaining onions, cilantro, ¼ cup of stock, poblanos, jalapeño, garlic, oregano, and cumin to a blender. Blend until coarsely pureed.

4. After 1 hour, reserve 1 cup of the hominy cooking liquid, then drain. Return the hominy to the Dutch oven along with the reserved liquid, chicken, blender sauce, remaining 1¾ cups of stock, and remaining ½ teaspoon of salt. Stir to combine.

5. Return to the stove and simmer over low heat. Cover and cook for 1 hour. Remove the chicken, let cool slightly, and pull the meat from the bones. Return it to the pot and let it warm back through.

SERVE IT WITH: Posole is often garnished with avocado slices and crunchy vegetables like shredded lettuce, diced red onion, or sliced radishes.

PER SERVING: Calories: 554; Total fat: 10g; Carbohydrates: 59g; Fiber: 5g; Protein: 55g; Sodium: 719mg

ROAST RACK OF LAMB AND BABY POTATOES (PAGE 89)

CHAPTER SIX

Everyday Decadence

When you're having company over, or maybe just have a little more time to spend on dinner, these recipes are sure to satisfy all desires. Remember, your Dutch oven isn't just for homey stews and quick pasta dinners. It can also star in a wide variety of elegant entrées, from sophisticated vegetarian dishes and stellar seafood recipes to decadent meat and chicken offerings. Whenever you're in the mood for something fancy, look no further.

FRENCH ONION SHORT RIBS

ACTIVE TIME: 20 minutes

TOTAL TIME: 2 hours

I adore French onion soup, and I also love *carbonnade flamande*. This recipe combines the two, with short ribs and lots of onions. Cooked in a sauce spiked with porter, the dish is finished by topping with bread and cheese. SERVES 4

2 teaspoons kosher
  salt, divided
2 pounds boneless
  short ribs
2 tablespoons
  vegetable oil
4 cups sliced onions
½ cup porter or other
  dark beer
2½ cups low-sodium
  beef broth
2 teaspoons
  Worcestershire sauce
1 teaspoon dried thyme or
  1 thyme sprig
3 cups stale bread cubes
  or croutons
1 cup grated Gruyère or
  Swiss cheese

PER SERVING: Calories: 742;
Total fat: 40g; Carbohydrates:
34g; Fiber: 3.5g; Protein: 57g;
Sodium: 1,151mg

1. Preheat the oven to 325°F.

2. Sprinkle 1½ teaspoons of the salt over the short ribs on all sides.

3. In a Dutch oven, heat the oil over medium heat. Add the short ribs and cook for 3 minutes. Flip and brown the other side for 3 minutes. Transfer to a plate.

4. Cook the onions with ¼ teaspoon of the salt in the pot for 5 to 6 minutes, until softened and lightly browned. Pour in the beer, scrape up the browned bits from the bottom, and cook for 3 to 4 minutes, until reduced by about one-third. Add the beef, broth, Worcestershire sauce, thyme, and remaining ¼ teaspoon of salt.

5. Place in the oven with the lid ajar. Cook for 90 minutes, or until the beef is tender. Remove from the oven and adjust the oven to 400°F.

6. Let sit for a few minutes, and skim off as much fat as possible. When the ribs have cooled, remove the ribs from the pot, trim any gristle, and return to the pot.

7. Spread the bread on top, then cover with the cheese.

8. Bake for 10 minutes, uncovered, until the cheese melts and the bread crisps.

SERVE IT WITH: A tangy green salad is all this dish needs to become a complete meal.

ROAST RACK of LAMB and BABY POTATOES

NUT-FREE

ACTIVE TIME: 25 minutes
TOTAL TIME: 45 minutes

This recipe pairs lamb racks with roasted potatoes and garlic for a truly elegant presentation. Don't worry about the amount of garlic—roasting makes it deliciously sweet and mellow. SERVES 4

2 (1¼ pound) racks of lamb, frenched

1½ teaspoons kosher salt, divided

3 tablespoons vegetable oil, divided

12 ounces baby potatoes

1 garlic head, plus 1 large peeled garlic clove, divided

2 English muffins, torn into 1-inch pieces

¼ cup fresh parsley leaves

½ teaspoon grated lemon zest

¼ teaspoon black pepper

1 teaspoon unsalted butter, melted

2 teaspoons Dijon-style mustard

PER SERVING: Calories: 460; Total fat: 21g; Carbohydrates: 29g; Fiber: 3.5g; Protein: 38g; Sodium: 699mg

1. Preheat oven to 375°F. Salt the lamb with 1 teaspoon of the salt.

2. In a Dutch oven, heat 1½ tablespoons of the oil over medium-high heat. When shimmering, place one lamb rack in the pot, meat-side down. Sear for about 2 minutes. Turn the rack to sear the ends. Repeat with the other rack. Set the racks aside.

3. Cut the head of garlic in half. Place in the pot along with the potatoes. Drizzle with the remaining 1½ tablespoons oil and ½ teaspoon salt, and toss to coat. Place in the oven, uncovered, and cook for 20 minutes.

4. In a food processor, mince the remaining garlic clove. Add the English muffins and parsley and process into coarse crumbs. Add the lemon zest, black pepper, and butter, and pulse to make a persillade.

5. Brush the meat side of each rack with mustard. Press the persillade over the meat.

6. Remove the pot from the oven. Toss the potatoes, and place the lamb racks on top. Roast for 20 to 25 minutes, until a meat thermometer registers 125°F.

7. Remove and let rest until the internal temperature has reached 135°F.

HELPFUL HINT: Depending on the size of your lamb racks, you may want to cut them into two pieces before coating with the crumb mixture.

BEEF STROGANOFF

NUT-FREE

ACTIVE TIME: 40 minutes
TOTAL TIME: 40 minutes

Growing up, I loved this quintessential company dish. Today, it's still a superb entrée—rich, beefy, and creamy—that comes together without much work. Serve over rice or egg noodles. SERVES 4

12 ounces sirloin tips, trimmed and cut into ⅛-inch-thick slices

1½ teaspoons kosher salt, divided

4 tablespoons (½ stick) unsalted butter, divided

1½ cups quartered cremini mushrooms

1 small onion, thinly sliced

3 tablespoons flour

⅓ cup cognac or brandy

1½ cups low-sodium beef stock

¼ cup sour cream

¼ teaspoon black pepper

1 tablespoon microgreens or chopped fresh dill

1. Sprinkle the beef with 1 teaspoon of the salt.

2. In a Dutch oven, heat 2 tablespoons of the butter until foaming. Sear the beef until browned, working in batches if necessary. Remove the beef and set aside.

3. Add the remaining 2 tablespoons of butter to the pot and heat until foaming. Add the mushrooms and ¼ teaspoon of the salt. Cook for 4 to 5 minutes, stirring occasionally, until the mushrooms begin to brown. Add the onion. Cook for about 3 minutes, stirring occasionally.

4. Sprinkle the vegetables with the flour and cook for 2 to 3 minutes, stirring, until the flour browns.

5. Remove the pot from the heat and add the cognac. Return to medium heat and scrape the bottom of the pot. When the cognac is mostly evaporated, add the stock and bring to a boil. Cook until thickened.

6. Reduce the heat to low, barely simmering. Stir in the sour cream, then the beef. Heat for a few minutes, until the sour cream is mixed in and the beef is warm. Stir in the remaining ¼ teaspoon of salt, if necessary, and the pepper.

7. When serving, garnish with microgreens.

SERVE IT WITH: Green Beans Amandine (page 107) is a good accompaniment, as is a green salad.

PER SERVING: Calories: 355; Total fat: 21g; Carbohydrates: 9g; Fiber: 0.5g; Protein: 20g; Sodium: 504mg

LOBSTER FRA DIAVOLO

ACTIVE TIME: 15 minutes

TOTAL TIME: 50 minutes

This streamlined version of a pasta classic uses lobster tails instead of the whole crustaceans and dresses them in a winning, spicy tomato sauce. **SERVES 4**

4 (6-ounce) lobster tails, thawed if frozen

1 tablespoon plus 1 teaspoon kosher salt, divided

12 ounces spaghetti

3 tablespoons olive oil

2 garlic cloves, sliced

1 teaspoon red pepper flakes

½ cup dry white wine

1 (28-ounce) can crushed tomatoes

2 teaspoons dried oregano

3 tablespoons chopped basil

1. In a Dutch oven, bring 1 inch of water to a boil. Place the lobster tails in a steamer basket, add to the pot, cover, and steam for 6 to 7 minutes, until the meat is opaque. Remove and let cool. Empty the pot.

2. In the Dutch oven, bring 3 quarts of water and 1 tablespoon of the salt to a boil. Add the spaghetti and cook according to package directions. Reserve 1 cup of pasta water, then drain.

3. In the Dutch oven, heat the oil over medium heat. Cook the garlic and red pepper flakes for 1 minute. Add the wine and cook for 2 to 3 minutes, until reduced by about half. Add the tomatoes, oregano, and remaining 1 teaspoon of salt and bring to a simmer. Cook, uncovered, for 15 to 20 minutes.

4. Meanwhile, using kitchen shears, cut down the middle of the lobster shells and pull apart. Remove the meat and cut into large chunks. Add to the sauce.

5. Pour the reserved pasta water over the spaghetti to loosen, then add it to the sauce. Stir gently and reheat for 1 to 2 minutes. Garnish with the basil.

EASY SUB: Large shrimp can stand in for the lobster in this recipe; just add them to the sauce to cook for a couple of minutes before adding the pasta in step 5.

PER SERVING: Calories: 618; Total fat: 13g; Carbohydrates: 79g; Fiber: 7.5g; Protein: 39g; Sodium: 1,604mg

ARTICHOKE and SPINACH GRATIN

NUT-FREE | VEGETARIAN

ACTIVE TIME: 15 minutes
TOTAL TIME: 45 minutes

Think of this dish as a deconstructed stuffed artichoke. It's way more sophisticated than the typical overrich spinach and artichoke dip, and it tastes much better, too. SERVES 4

4 tablespoons (½ stick) unsalted butter, divided

1 pound baby spinach

½ teaspoon kosher salt

3 cups frozen artichoke hearts, thawed

½ teaspoon dried Italian herbs

¼ cup heavy cream

½ cup whole-milk ricotta cheese

⅔ cup panko bread crumbs

⅓ cup grated Parmesan cheese

1. Preheat the oven to 375°F.

2. In a Dutch oven, melt 2 tablespoons of the butter over medium heat until foaming. Add the spinach by big handfuls and stir to wilt, continuing to add handfuls until all the spinach is wilted. Sprinkle with the salt and stir.

3. Add the artichoke hearts and Italian herbs and simmer for 8 to 10 minutes, or until the spinach liquid has mostly evaporated. Drizzle with the cream. Dot the surface with 1-tablespoon scoops of ricotta.

4. In the microwave or a small saucepan, melt the remaining 2 tablespoons of butter. Add the bread crumbs and stir. Let cool for a few minutes, then add the Parmesan cheese. Sprinkle the bread crumb mixture evenly over the top.

5. Bake, uncovered, for 15 to 20 minutes, or until bubbling and browned on top.

EASY SUB: Frozen artichokes have a better flavor than those in jars or cans, but the canned variety can be used if you can't find frozen ones. Just rinse well and drain before using.

PER SERVING: Calories: 372; Total fat: 23g; Carbohydrates: 28g; Fiber: 11g; Protein: 13g; Sodium: 766mg

CRAB and ASPARAGUS RISOTTO

GLUTEN-FREE NUT-FREE

ACTIVE TIME: 15 minutes
TOTAL TIME: 45 minutes

Risotto has the reputation of being finicky and requiring constant supervision, but it's easy once you get the hang of it. If you can find fresh crab, it's wonderful, but pasteurized refrigerated crab is just fine. **SERVES 4**

1 pound asparagus, cut into 1½-inch lengths

6 cups low-sodium chicken or vegetable broth

6 tablespoons (¾ stick) unsalted butter, divided

2 shallots, minced

1½ cups Arborio or carnaroli rice

½ teaspoon kosher salt

½ cup dry white wine

¼ cup grated Parmesan cheese

8 ounces fresh or pasteurized refrigerated crabmeat

1. In a Dutch oven, bring an inch of water to a boil. Place the asparagus in a steamer basket, add to the pot, and cover to steam for 4 to 5 minutes, or until tender. Remove from the pot and pour out the water.

2. In a saucepan, heat the broth and keep warm.

3. In a Dutch oven, melt 3 tablespoons of the butter over medium heat until foaming. Add the shallots and cook, stirring, until softened slightly. Add the rice and salt and stir. Add the wine and bring to a simmer. Cook for 2 to 3 minutes, until the wine has almost evaporated.

4. Add 1 cup of the broth and stir until it has been mostly absorbed by the rice. Continue to add broth, 1 cup at a time, as the broth is absorbed. Stir regularly. After about 25 minutes, check the rice for doneness (tender but firm in the center), adding additional broth and cooking more if necessary.

5. Add the remaining 3 tablespoons of butter and Parmesan and stir to melt. Fold in the crab and asparagus to warm before serving.

EASY SUB: Try smoked salmon or sautéed shrimp instead of the crab, or mushrooms instead of the asparagus.

PER SERVING: Calories: 561; Total fat: 20g; Carbohydrates: 70g; Fiber: 5.5g; Protein: 23g; Sodium: 689mg

WILD MUSHROOM "WELLINGTON"

NUT-FREE **VEGETARIAN**

ACTIVE TIME: 15 minutes
TOTAL TIME: 45 minutes

Beef Wellington is tenderloin of beef with a layer of mushrooms wrapped in puff pastry. Skip the beef, and the hassle of wrapping, and you'll have this easy, festive, delicious vegetarian entrée. SERVES 4

3 tablespoons unsalted butter, divided

1 pound mixed wild mushrooms, chopped

2 shallots, minced

2 teaspoons kosher salt, divided

1 tablespoon chopped fresh parsley

2 teaspoons fresh thyme leaves or 1 teaspoon dried thyme

¼ cup dry sherry

½ cup heavy cream

4 large portabella mushrooms, stems and gills removed

1 puff pastry sheet

1 egg, beaten

1. Preheat the oven to 375°F.

2. In a Dutch oven, melt 1½ tablespoons of the butter over medium heat until foaming. Add the mushrooms and shallots and sprinkle with 1 teaspoon of the salt. Cook, stirring occasionally, until most of the liquid has evaporated.

3. Stir in the parsley and thyme. Pour in the sherry and bring to a simmer. Cook until it has reduced by half, then add the cream. Bring back to a simmer and cook for 2 to 3 minutes, until thickened.

4. Sprinkle the insides of the portabellas with the remaining 1 teaspoon of salt. Scoop the mushroom mixture into the portabellas. Wipe out the pot and add the remaining 1½ tablespoons of butter. When it foams, add the portabellas, filled-side up.

5. Roll out the puff pastry lightly and cut into 4 squares. Top each portabella with a square of pastry and brush with the egg wash.

6. Place in the oven and bake, uncovered, for 25 to 30 minutes, or until the pastry is puffed and deep golden brown.

SERVE IT WITH: Green Beans Amandine (page 107) or Italian Braised Zucchini (page 105) goes well with the mushrooms.

PER SERVING: Calories: 514; Total fat: 36g; Carbohydrates: 45g; Fiber: 4.5g; Protein: 12g; Sodium: 813mg

STUFFED BACON-WRAPPED PORK TENDERLOIN

ACTIVE TIME: 20 minutes
TOTAL TIME: 55 minutes

Since pork tenderloin is a lean cut, it benefits from a covering of bacon (avoid thick-cut slices) while it cooks, resulting in juicy meat with a crisp exterior. Cherries are the star in the flavorful stuffing. SERVES 4

1 (1½ pounds)
   pork tenderloin
1½ teaspoons kosher
   salt, divided
½ cup apple cider
2 tablespoons
   cider vinegar
¾ cup dried cherries
1 tablespoon vegetable oil
1 shallot, minced
1 garlic clove, minced
½ cup fresh bread crumbs
1 teaspoon dried thyme
4 to 6 slices bacon
   or prosciutto

PER SERVING: Calories: 480;
Total fat: 21g; Carbohydrates:
33g; Fiber: 2g; Protein: 42g;
Sodium: 779mg

1. Preheat the oven to 375°F.

2. Sprinkle the pork with 1 teaspoon of the salt (if your tenderloin is brined, omit).

3. In the microwave or a small pot, bring the apple cider and vinegar to a simmer. Add the cherries and set aside to rehydrate.

4. In a Dutch oven, heat the oil over medium heat. When it shimmers, add the shallot and garlic and cook for 1 to 2 minutes, or until softened and fragrant. Add the bread crumbs, thyme, and remaining ½ teaspoon of salt, and stir. Pour the cherries and liquid into the pot and stir.

5. Cut the tenderloin lengthwise to about ½ inch from the side so you can open it up like a book. Spread the cherry stuffing over half of the tenderloin and fold the other half over. Wrap the tenderloin with strips of bacon, securing the bacon with toothpicks. Cut the tenderloin in half so it will fit in the Dutch oven.

6. Place the pot in the oven, uncovered, and roast for 15 minutes. Remove the pot and turn the pork over. Roast for another 12 to 15 minutes, or until the internal temperature registers 140°F to 145°F.

SERVE IT WITH: Italian Braised Zucchini (page 105) makes a great first course for the pork.

FISH and VEGETABLES with CHERMOULA

ACTIVE TIME: 15 minutes
TOTAL TIME: 1 hour

Chermoula is a spicy Moroccan herb sauce with tangy lemon to balance the garlic and spices. It makes a delicious accent to the mild fish and vegetables.
SERVES 4

4 garlic cloves, peeled

1 cup fresh cilantro leaves

1 cup fresh parsley leaves

¼ cup lemon juice

2½ teaspoons kosher
    salt, divided

1¼ teaspoons
    sweet paprika

¼ teaspoon ground cumin

¼ teaspoon
    ground cayenne

3 tablespoons olive oil

4 (5-ounce) tilapia, cod,
    or snapper fillets

Nonstick cooking spray

2 cups peeled Yukon
    Gold potatoes, cut into
    ¼-inch-thick slices

½ red bell pepper,
    seeded and cut into
    bite-size chunks

½ green bell pepper,
    seeded and cut into
    bite-size chunks

1 small onion, sliced

1 large tomato, seeded
    and cut into chunks

1. To make the chermoula, in a food processor, mince the garlic. Add the cilantro, parsley, lemon juice, 1½ teaspoons of the salt, paprika, cumin, and cayenne, and process until mostly smooth. With the processor running, drizzle in the oil and process until incorporated.

2. Preheat the oven to 400°F.

3. Sprinkle the fish on both sides with the remaining 1 teaspoon of salt and brush with 2 tablespoons of chermoula. Place the fish in the refrigerator.

4. Meanwhile, coat a Dutch oven with cooking spray. Toss the potatoes with 3 tablespoons of chermoula, and arrange evenly in the pot. Cover and bake for 15 minutes.

5. As the potatoes are cooking, toss the bell peppers and onion with 2 tablespoons of chermoula. Place the peppers and onion over the potatoes. Cover and bake for 15 minutes.

6. Remove from the oven. Spoon the tomato chunks over the peppers and onions and place the fish fillets on top. Drizzle the remaining chermoula over the top. Cover and bake for 15 minutes.

HELPFUL HINT: If you don't have a food processor, finely mince the herbs and garlic and whisk the sauce together.

PER SERVING: Calories: 337; Total fat: 17g; Carbohydrates: 19g; Fiber: 3.5g; Protein: 31g; Sodium: 802mg

CHICKEN SALTIMBOCCA

NUT-FREE

ACTIVE TIME: 30 minutes
TOTAL TIME: 30 minutes

In this version, chicken stands in for the traditional veal and is layered with salty prosciutto and sage leaves to make for an impressive entrée. SERVES 4

2 (8-ounce) large
   boneless, skinless
   chicken breasts
2 teaspoons kosher salt
¼ teaspoon black pepper
⅔ cup flour
5 tablespoons olive
   oil, divided
4 large, thin
   slices prosciutto
8 to 10 sage leaves
¼ cup dry white wine
2 tablespoons
   unsalted butter
2 teaspoons lemon juice

PER SERVING: Calories: 416;
Total fat: 27g; Carbohydrates: 9g;
Fiber: 0g; Protein: 31g;
Sodium: 987mg

1. Holding your knife parallel to the cutting board, slice the chicken breasts in half so you have 4 pieces about ½ inch thick. Using the heel of your hand, press to even out the thickness. Sprinkle with the salt and pepper and dredge with the flour.

2. Working in batches, in a Dutch oven, heat 2 tablespoons of the oil over medium-high heat. Add half the chicken and cook for 2 to 3 minutes per side, until golden brown. Repeat with 2 tablespoons of oil and the remaining chicken. Set aside.

3. In the Dutch oven, heat the remaining 1 tablespoon of oil. One at a time, add a slice of prosciutto and cook for 30 seconds. Place the slice on top of a chicken piece, and repeat with the remaining slices. Place the chicken on a baking sheet in the oven set to its lowest temperature to keep warm.

4. Add the sage leaves to the pot and cook for 1 to 2 minutes, stirring. Add the wine and cook for 3 to 4 minutes, stirring to get up any browned bits. Turn the heat off and swirl in the butter, 1 tablespoon at a time, to make a smooth sauce. Add the lemon juice.

5. Transfer the chicken breasts to a serving platter and top with the sauce.

SERVE IT WITH: Silky Garlic Mashed Potatoes (page 109) or Roasted Red Pepper Polenta (page 112) would complement the chicken nicely.

GERMAN POTATO SALAD (PAGE 113)

CHAPTER SEVEN

Quick Sides

By now, you've figured out all the great entrées and meals you can make in your Dutch oven. But it's also great for side dishes, and the recipes in this chapter will show you how to complete your dinner menus to perfection. They can all be made completely or partly ahead of time and easily reheated or finished later, so they'll fit in with the busiest of dinner schedules.

SCALLOPED SWEET POTATOES

GLUTEN-FREE | **NUT-FREE** | **VEGETARIAN**

ACTIVE TIME: 15 minutes
TOTAL TIME: 40 minutes

While less common than russets or Yukon Gold potatoes, a gratin with sweet potatoes is a wonderful, elegant side dish. In this version, they simmer in a savory cream sauce before being topped with cheese and browned in the oven. **SERVES 4**

1 cup heavy cream

½ cup whole milk

3 garlic cloves, peeled and crushed

1 sprig rosemary

2 medium sweet potatoes

1½ teaspoons kosher salt

¼ teaspoon black pepper

¾ cup grated Parmesan cheese

1. In a Dutch oven, combine the cream and milk. Add the garlic and rosemary. Bring to a simmer over medium-low heat.

2. While the sauce simmers, peel the sweet potatoes and cut into ¼-inch-thick slices.

3. Remove the rosemary sprig and garlic cloves from the cream mixture. Stir in the salt and pepper. Add the sweet potatoes and stir to cover with the cream.

4. Keeping the cream at a simmer, cook the sweet potato slices for 8 to 10 minutes, or until just starting to soften.

5. While the potatoes cook, preheat the oven to 425°F.

6. Sprinkle the cheese over the sweet potatoes. Transfer the pot to the oven and bake for about 20 minutes, uncovered, until the sweet potatoes are tender, the sauce is bubbling, and the cheese is browned. If the cheese is not browned, turn on the broiler for a couple of minutes.

HELPFUL HINT: You can prep part of this recipe ahead of time by cooking the potatoes in step 4, then letting cool; cover the Dutch oven and refrigerate for up to 3 days. To finish cooking, sprinkle with cheese and bake for 30 to 40 minutes, or until sauce is bubbling.

PER SERVING: Calories: 339; Total fat: 26g; Carbohydrates: 19g; Fiber: 2g; Protein: 8g; Sodium: 756mg

HERBED RICE PILAF

GLUTEN-FREE NUT-FREE

ACTIVE TIME: 10 minutes
TOTAL TIME: 30 minutes

This deliciously easy side is a great way to use up any herbs you might have in the fridge. Parsley and dill make a nice combination, or use cilantro and basil for a taste of Southeast Asia. SERVES 4

3 tablespoons
   unsalted butter
½ cup chopped onion
¼ cup chopped red
   bell pepper
1 garlic clove, minced
1 cup long-grain white rice
1¾ cups low-sodium
   chicken or vegetable
   stock
½ teaspoon kosher salt
3 tablespoons minced
   fresh herbs

1. In a Dutch oven, heat the butter over medium heat until foaming. Add the onion, bell pepper, and garlic and cook for 3 to 5 minutes, until the onion is soft and translucent. Add the rice and stir to coat.

2. Add the stock and salt. Bring to a boil, then reduce the heat as low as it can get and cover the pot. Cook for 20 minutes. The liquid should be almost completely absorbed, and the rice should be tender but not gummy.

3. Gently stir in the herbs. Cover the pot and let rest for another 5 minutes. Fluff with a fork before serving.

HELPFUL HINT: It's nice to have a few make-ahead sides ready to go before the start of the workweek. Cook through step 2, let cool, and store. To finish, return the rice to the Dutch oven and heat the rice over low heat, adding a few tablespoons of stock if rice is too dry. Stir in the herbs and let sit for a minute.

PER SERVING: Calories: 270; Total fat: 9g; Carbohydrates: 40g; Fiber: 1g; Protein: 6g; Sodium: 175mg

SOUTHWESTERN CREAMED CORN

ACTIVE TIME: 10 minutes
TOTAL TIME: 35 minutes

If your idea of creamed corn is the gloppy stuff in cans, you'll be pleasantly surprised by this light, creamy version laced with spices and green chiles. It's a wonderful accompaniment to any Southwestern or Tex-Mex entrée, such as Chorizo-Stuffed Peppers (page 38). **SERVES 4**

2 tablespoons
  unsalted butter

2 cups frozen corn, thawed

½ medium onion, diced

1 teaspoon kosher salt

½ teaspoon chili powder

¼ teaspoon ground cumin

⅛ teaspoon ground
  cayenne

½ cup heavy cream

1 (4-ounce) can diced
  green chiles

1. In a Dutch oven, melt the butter over medium heat until foaming. Add the corn and onion and cook, stirring occasionally, for about 5 minutes, until the onion softens and becomes translucent.

2. Stir in the salt, chili powder, cumin, and cayenne. Add the cream and reduce the heat to medium-low. Cover and cook, stirring occasionally, for 20 minutes.

3. Stir in the chiles and their juices and continue to cook until the corn is tender and the cream has thickened slightly.

HELPFUL HINT: Got leftovers? The corn mixture can thicken overnight, so, if necessary, add another tablespoon or so of cream while reheating.

PER SERVING: Calories: 227; Total fat: 18g; Carbohydrates: 17g; Fiber: 2g; Protein: 4g; Sodium: 413mg

ITALIAN BRAISED ZUCCHINI

DAIRY-FREE | **GLUTEN-FREE** | **NUT-FREE** | **VEGETARIAN**

ACTIVE TIME:
10 minutes
TOTAL TIME: 30 minutes

When I was growing up, my dad always had a huge vegetable garden with lots of zucchini. Mom got very creative using it all, and this combination of zucchini, tomatoes, and herbs was one of our favorites. SERVES 4

2 tablespoons olive oil

1 small onion, sliced

1 teaspoon kosher salt

2 large zucchini, cut into ½-inch-thick slices

1 medium tomato, diced

2 garlic cloves, minced

½ teaspoon dried oregano

½ teaspoon dried basil

¼ teaspoon black pepper

1. In a Dutch oven, heat the oil over medium heat until shimmering. Add the onion and salt. Cook, stirring, for 1 to 2 minutes, or until beginning to soften. Add the zucchini, tomato, garlic, oregano, basil, and black pepper and stir.

2. Raise the heat to medium-high. Cover the pot and cook for 10 to 12 minutes, or until the vegetables are tender.

HELPFUL HINT: You can prepare part of this recipe a day or two before you plan to eat it. Simply cook the vegetables until they're becoming tender, about 6 minutes. Let cool, then cover and refrigerate up to 3 days. Return the vegetables to the Dutch oven, reheat gently to finish cooking, then serve.

PER SERVING: Calories: 102; Total fat: 7.5g; Carbohydrates: 8g; Fiber: 2g; Protein: 2g; Sodium: 295mg

GREEN BEANS AMANDINE

ACTIVE TIME: 18 minutes
TOTAL TIME: 18 minutes

I learned to make green beans with almonds back in college, and for years it was my go-to vegetable for company. It's easy, but delicious and fancy enough for guests. SERVES 6

1 pound green
   beans, trimmed
2 tablespoons olive oil or
   unsalted butter, divided
⅓ cup sliced or
   slivered almonds
½ teaspoon kosher salt
1 teaspoon grated
   lemon zest

1. In a Dutch oven, bring an inch of water to a boil. Place the beans in a steamer basket. When the water boils, place the steamer in the pot. Cover the pot and cook the beans for 4 minutes, or until they start to become tender. Remove the steamer from the pot and pour out the water. Set the green beans aside.

2. In the Dutch oven, heat 1 tablespoon of the oil over medium heat. When it's hot, add the almonds and cook for 3 to 4 minutes, stirring constantly, until golden brown. Using a slotted spoon, transfer the nuts to a bowl.

3. Add the remaining 1 tablespoon of oil to the pot. When it's hot, add the green beans and salt and cook, stirring occasionally, for 5 to 6 minutes, or until the beans are tender. Stir in the almonds and lemon zest and serve immediately.

HELPFUL HINT: To split up some of the cooking, steam the beans in step 1 and let cool. Refrigerate until ready to use, up to 3 days. Brown the almonds and let cool. When ready to serve, return the beans to the Dutch oven and continue with step 3.

PER SERVING: Calories: 93; Total fat: 7g; Carbohydrates: 6g; Fiber: 2.5g; Protein: 3g; Sodium: 98mg

SMOKY REFRIED BEANS

DAIRY-FREE | GLUTEN-FREE | NUT-FREE

ACTIVE TIME: 10 minutes
TOTAL TIME: 30 minutes

Refritos are one of my favorite Mexican dishes. Cooked and mashed into bacon fat, they turn into a creamy, super-flavorful side dish that's perfect for any entrée inspired by cuisines south of the border. SERVES 4

2 (15-ounce) cans
   pinto beans
½ small onion, root
   left intact
3 thick bacon
   slices, diced
½ teaspoon
   ground cumin
½ teaspoon
   ground chipotle

1. In a Dutch oven, combine the beans and their liquid and the onion. Bring to a simmer over medium heat. Cover and cook for 20 minutes, or until very soft.

2. Remove the onion. Pour the beans into a strainer set over a bowl, reserving the liquid.

3. Return the Dutch oven to the heat and add the bacon. Cook for 6 to 8 minutes, stirring, until the fat has rendered and the bacon is becoming crisp. Transfer the bacon to a paper towel, leaving the fat in the pot. Crumble the bacon.

4. Raise the heat to medium-high. Add the beans and a few spoonfuls of their liquid to the pot. Using a potato masher, mash into a coarse paste, adding more liquid as necessary. Stir in the cumin and chipotle. Sprinkle the bacon over just before serving.

HELPFUL HINT: These beans are great made ahead of time. They may firm up somewhat; if so, just add a little stock or water to loosen. Add the bacon right before serving so it stays crisp.

PER SERVING: Calories: 249; Total fat: 9.5g; Carbohydrates: 29g; Fiber: 8g; Protein: 12g; Sodium: 470mg

SILKY GARLIC MASHED POTATOES

GLUTEN-FREE | **NUT-FREE** | **VEGETARIAN**

ACTIVE TIME: 10 minutes
TOTAL TIME: 30 minutes

I've cooked potatoes for mashing any number of ways, from pressure cooking to boiling to baking. My favorite method, by far, is steaming. Using a potato ricer produces the smoothest puree, but if you don't have one, a potato masher will also work. **SERVES 6**

2 pounds russet potatoes, peeled and cut into 3-inch chunks

6 large garlic cloves, peeled

¾ cup heavy cream

6 tablespoons (¾ stick) unsalted butter, cut into 4 pieces

1¼ teaspoons kosher salt

1. In a Dutch oven, bring an inch of water to a boil. Place the potatoes and garlic in a steamer basket. When the water boils, place the steamer in the pot. Cover and cook for 15 to 18 minutes, or until the potatoes are very soft. Remove the steamer from the pot and pour out the water.

2. Place the Dutch oven over very low heat and add the cream. A few at a time, pass the potato chunks and garlic through a potato ricer into the pot. Add the butter and salt and stir to combine and melt the butter. Add more cream, if necessary, to make a smooth puree.

HELPFUL HINT: Like most starches, mashed potatoes will thicken when refrigerated. For leftovers, reheat over very low heat, stirring occasionally and adding more cream, if necessary, for the right consistency.

PER SERVING: Calories: 321; Total fat: 22g; Carbohydrates: 28g; Fiber: 2g; Protein: 4g; Sodium: 244mg

CRISPY ONION RINGS

NUT-FREE VEGETARIAN

ACTIVE TIME: 40 minutes

TOTAL TIME: 40 minutes

No doubt about it—these onion rings are a labor of love. But if you have the time and don't mind a bit of mess, they are *so* worth it. The rice flour helps keep them super crisp, so the first batch is just as crunchy as the last. SERVES 6

2 medium sweet onions

2 cups buttermilk

1 egg

8 cups vegetable oil

2 cups all-purpose flour

2 cups rice flour
  or cornstarch

2 teaspoons
  baking powder

1 teaspoon table salt

PER SERVING: Calories: 509;
Total fat: 12g; Carbohydrates:
91g; Fiber: 2g; Protein: 7g;
Sodium: 410mg

1. Trim the onions and cut them into 1/4-inch slices. Separate the slices into rings.

2. In a wide, flat bowl, whisk together the buttermilk and egg. Place the onion rings in the mixture, submerging them as much as possible.

3. In a Dutch oven, heat the oil over medium-low heat until it reaches 360°F.

4. While the oil is heating, place the flours and baking powder in a large, heavy plastic bag. Seal it and shake to combine.

5. About a quarter at a time, transfer the rings to the bag. Seal and shake to coat the rings.

6. When the oil is hot, transfer the rings to the Dutch oven, using tongs to separate them. Fry for 3 to 4 minutes, stirring, until golden brown. Transfer to a rack placed over a baking sheet, arranging them in a single layer. Move the pot to a warming drawer or a warm oven.

7. Repeat with the remaining onions, letting the oil return to 360°F between batches. Just before serving, sprinkle evenly with the salt.

HELPFUL HINT: These are best eaten right away, but they do reheat surprisingly well. Keep them on the rack and cover lightly with a sheet of foil or paper towels, then refrigerate. Reheat in a 300°F oven for 10 to 12 minutes, or until hot.

ROASTED RED PEPPER POLENTA

GLUTEN-FREE | NUT-FREE

ACTIVE TIME: 10 minutes
TOTAL TIME: 40 minutes

If you've never made polenta or grits from scratch, you might be intimidated; there's a lot of hype about how difficult it is. But in truth, if you have enough liquid and cook the mixture slowly, you've got nothing to worry about. Avoid using instant or quick-cook grains. SERVES 4

2 cups low-sodium
  chicken stock
2 cups whole milk
1 tablespoon
  unsalted butter
1 teaspoon kosher salt
1 cup polenta or grits
½ cup grated
  cheddar cheese
½ cup chopped canned
  roasted red peppers

1. In a Dutch oven, heat the stock, milk, butter, and salt over medium heat. Whisk in the polenta.

2. Bring to a boil and continue to stir.

3. Reduce the heat to low and cover the pot. Keep the grits at a light simmer and cook for 30 minutes, stirring occasionally and adding more stock or water if it becomes too thick.

4. Stir in the cheese and peppers.

HELPFUL HINT: Polenta will set up when refrigerated but will soften when reheated. Stir in a couple of tablespoons milk or stock and reheat slowly, stirring to break up clumps. Or, pour it into a shallow pan and refrigerate, then cut into squares and fry them.

PER SERVING: Calories: 283; Total fat: 9g; Carbohydrates: 35g; Fiber: 2g; Protein: 13g; Sodium: 488mg

GERMAN POTATO SALAD

ACTIVE TIME: 10 minutes
TOTAL TIME: 25 minutes

There are a couple of styles of German potato salad; this one is my favorite. Instead of a cold salad with a mayonnaise-based sauce, this is served warm, with a bacon and mustard vinaigrette. It's absolutely delicious! **SERVES 4**

1 pound baby or fingerling potatoes, halved

4 tablespoons cider vinegar, divided

¼ teaspoon kosher salt

3 thick bacon slices, chopped

½ cup chopped onion

1 small celery stalk, chopped

1 tablespoon whole-grain mustard

2 teaspoons granulated sugar

¼ teaspoon celery seeds

1 tablespoon chopped fresh dill or parsley

1. In a Dutch oven, bring an inch of water to a boil. Place the potatoes in a steamer basket. When the water boils, place the steamer in the pot. Cover and cook the potatoes for 10 to 14 minutes, or until tender. Remove the steamer basket from the pot. Transfer the potatoes to a bowl and sprinkle with 1 tablespoon of the vinegar and the salt. Toss gently. Pour the water out of the Dutch oven.

2. In the Dutch oven, cook the bacon over medium heat, stirring, for about 4 minutes, or until mostly crisp. Transfer to a paper towel, leaving the fat in the pot.

3. Add the onion and celery. Cook, stirring, for 1 minute, then add the remaining 3 tablespoons vinegar, mustard, sugar, and celery seeds. Stir to dissolve the sugar.

4. Pour the dressing over the potatoes and add the reserved bacon and dill. Toss gently.

HELPFUL HINT: While the salad is best served warm, it's still good the next day if brought to room temperature before serving.

PER SERVING: Calories: 188; Total fat: 8.5g; Carbohydrates: 23g; Fiber: 3.5g; Protein: 5g; Sodium: 309mg

MEASUREMENT CONVERSIONS

VOLUME EQUIVALENTS	U.S. STANDARD	U.S. STANDARD (OUNCES)	METRIC (APPROXIMATE)
LIQUID	2 tablespoons	1 fl. oz.	30 mL
	¼ cup	2 fl. oz.	60 mL
	½ cup	4 fl. oz.	120 mL
	1 cup	8 fl. oz.	240 mL
	1½ cups	12 fl. oz.	355 mL
	2 cups or 1 pint	16 fl. oz.	475 mL
	4 cups or 1 quart	32 fl. oz.	1 L
	1 gallon	128 fl. oz.	4 L
DRY	⅛ teaspoon	—	0.5 mL
	¼ teaspoon	—	1 mL
	½ teaspoon	—	2 mL
	¾ teaspoon	—	4 mL
	1 teaspoon	—	5 mL
	1 tablespoon	—	15 mL
	¼ cup	—	59 mL
	⅓ cup	—	79 mL
	½ cup	—	118 mL
	⅔ cup	—	156 mL
	¾ cup	—	177 mL
	1 cup	—	235 mL
	2 cups or 1 pint	—	475 mL
	3 cups	—	700 mL
	4 cups or 1 quart	—	1 L
	½ gallon	—	2 L
	1 gallon	—	4 L

OVEN TEMPERATURES

FAHRENHEIT	CELSIUS (APPROXIMATE)
250°F	120°C
300°F	150°C
325°F	165°C
350°F	180°C
375°F	190°C
400°F	200°C
425°F	220°C
450°F	230°C

WEIGHT EQUIVALENTS

U.S. STANDARD	METRIC (APPROXIMATE)
½ ounce	15 g
1 ounce	30 g
2 ounces	60 g
4 ounces	115 g
8 ounces	225 g
12 ounces	340 g
16 ounces or 1 pound	455 g

RECIPE INDEX

INDEX

ACKNOWLEDGMENTS

Thanks to the team at Callisto, especially Lauren Ladoceour and Elizabeth Castoria. And special thanks to my sister Eileen for her valuable advice.

ABOUT THE AUTHOR

 JANET A. ZIMMERMAN is the award-winning author of eight previous cookbooks, including *All-in-One Dutch Oven Cookbook for Two* and the best-selling *Instant Pot Obsession*. She's been writing about food and teaching students to cook for almost 20 years. She lives and cooks with her partner, Dave, and a shelf full of Dutch ovens in Atlanta.

CPSIA information can be obtained
at www.ICGtesting.com
Printed in the USA
JSHW020712150920
7910JS00002B/2